The HELICOPTER STORY
of the FALKLANDS CAMPAIGN

The HELICOPTER STORY of the FALKLANDS CAMPAIGN

John Hamilton

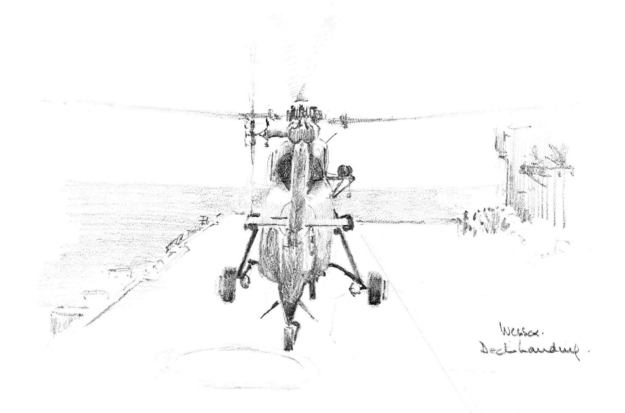

Wessex.
Deck Landing.

DAVID & CHARLES
Newton Abbot   London

King Edwards Point
South Georgia 1988

British Library Cataloguing in Publication Data
Hamilton, John
    The helicopter story of the Falklands campaign.
    1. Falkland Islands War. Air operations by British
    military forces. Helicopters
    I. Title
    997.11
    ISBN 0–7153–9286–7

Book designed by Michael Head

Typeset by Ace Filmsetting Ltd, Frome, Somerset
and printed in Singapore
by CS Graphics Pte Ltd
for David & Charles Publishers plc
Brunel House, Newton Abbot, Devon

List of Paintings

List of abbreviations

AA	Anti aircraft	Para	Paratrooper or Paratroop Battalion
AAC	Army Air Corps	PNG	Passive Night Goggles (image intensifying goggles)
AEW	Airborne Early Warning		
ASW	Anti Submarine Warning	RA	Royal Artillery
Bn.	Battalion	RAF	Royal Air Force
CASEVAC	Casualty Evacuation	RAS	Replenishment at Sea
CBAS	Commando Brigade Air Squadron	RM	Royal Marine
ESM	Electronic Support (or surveillance) Measures	SAS	Special Air Service
		SBS	Special Boat Section
GPMG	General Purpose Machine Gun	TEZ	Total Exclusion Zone (an area with a radius of two hundred miles round the Falkland Islands)
HDS	Helicopter Delivery Service		
NASA	National Aeronautics and Space Administration (US)		
		VERTREP	Vertical replenishment
NGS	Naval Gun Support		

Acknowledgements

The historical painter and storyteller must draw on the labours of others whose published works are essential to his research. I am indeed grateful for the help I have received from many sources, and in particular from:

The Air War published by Arms and Armour Press, *The Royal Navy in the Falklands War* by David Brown, the essential helicopter details from many publications published by Ian Allen, and also Mike Critchley's small books which are packed with detailed information. Of the many other detailed works I am indebted to Martin Middlebrook for his *Task Force* and *Fight for the Malvinas*, and to Max Hastings and Simon Jenkins for their *Battle for the Falklands*, Roger Perkins' *Operation Paraquot* and of course to the many people who have loaned me photographs and slides. The Photographic Units of the Royal Navy, the Royal Marines and Westlands gave me all the help I asked for. To all these people and to many more I offer my thanks.

A corner of San Carlos Cemetry
The Graves of Captain Dent, Private Slough
and Staff Sergeant Baker — all of the Parachute
Regiment.

Feb 8/88.

Introduction

This is a story, not a history, and it is a story in paint. To present anything else would require a balanced picture of both sides of the conflict, which I have not attempted, but the helicopter story of the Falklands campaign is nonetheless remarkable. In this book I have endeavoured to illustrate just one aspect of the 74-day campaign, of which only 25 days were on land in the Falkland Islands, requiring the transport of men and weapons of war nearly 8,000 miles out and 8,000 miles home.

Our story starts on 2 April and ends on 14 June 1982. It was something of a freak of history; to the Victorians, colonial wars were nothing new and the country came to accept as normal a heavy casualty list caused as much by disease as by battle, but that would be unthinkable today. It was with a feeling of unreal shock that the British people in 1982 realised that the country was at war. From then on the minute-by-minute activities of the Task Force swept all else from television screens and newspapers alike in a way that was far more immediate than all the horrors of forty years before. Violence all over the world, and particularly the troubles in Northern Ireland, had conditioned the readers and viewers of the 1980s to demand instant information and comment.

Much has been written since, and hosts of photographs have illustrated all aspects of the conflict, so why another book on the subject? The reason is that the helicopter story has never really been told, despite the fact that it was crucial to the whole campaign. As it was, with the aircraft available, it was a 'close run thing'. Had the professional standard of maintenance been less than outstanding, and a significant number of aircraft been grounded as a result, then the campaign itself would have ground to a halt. The loss of the *Atlantic Conveyor* with its cargo of Chinook and Wessex helicopters was a blow which was to deprive the Land Force Commander of much-needed flexibility during the landing and subsequent advance to retake the island.

This book is an attempt to tell that story. Behind the headlines of outstanding feats of flying are stories of equally outstanding devotion to duty and professionalism by ground staff and maintenance crews. It was the maintainers who kept the aircraft flying and gave the operations staff the maximum number to deploy to the best advantage. But what of the aircraft themselves? The makers' specifications were exceeded in all respects. In the stress of operational situations they carried far heavier loads than they were designed for. They flew longer and further, at times without normal maintenance, and the credit for this must lie in the design and manufacture by Westlands of Yeovil who built nearly all the helicopters deployed with the Task Force and at Ascension Island.

Let me stress again that this book is about helicopters and for that reason I have omitted other aspects of the conflict in which they were not involved to any major degree. There are a number of fine paintings which depict the actions of men and ships, however; it is perhaps a pity that they have not as yet been brought together to have wider publicity.

This book would not have been possible without the generous help of many people. In the Royal Navy, to the Flag Officer Naval Air Command, the Director of the Fleet Air Arm Museum and the Commanding Officer of HMS *Endurance*, and to their staff, I owe a special debt. In the Falkland Islands, the Commander of British Forces and the Senior Naval Officer made it possible for me to visit places of historic interest, and both the Army Air Corps and 78 Squadron RAF ensured that the visits took place. I was made welcome on Rapier sites and outposts all over the islands, just as I was as a guest of the islanders. It is impossible to mention everyone and I hope that they will all accept my thanks.

A historian is judged by his accuracy and by his sense of balance, and I believe that a historical painter must be judged in exactly the same way. Despite careful checking with those who were there at the time, I am sure that the reader will find numerous faults and omissions. Those faults and those omissions lie at my door. I should also mention that I feel strongly that it becomes invidious to mention individuals by name, for behind every action in the campaign – whether at sea, on the ground or in the air – there was a complete team effort. Thus the reader will notice the absence of named individuals, and in their place the name of the squadron or ship or unit involved.

Finally a personal word. I suggested to my publishers that they should publish this book to a high specification. This was readily agreed, but it was pointed out that inevitably the costs would escalate. All along I have wanted *The Helicopter Story* to be available at a price which all ranks of the Services, the Royal Fleet Auxiliary, the Merchant Navy and all those who built the aircraft could afford. I put the problem to Westlands and they readily agreed most generously to subsidise the considerable financial shortfall. For this gesture I am extremely grateful; at the same time it is a privilege to be able to record a story so intimately linked with British inventive craftsmanship, of which that company and this country may be justly proud.

JOHN HAMILTON
The Studio
Tresco
Isles of Scilly
Cornwall
February 1990

Foreword

Sir John Treacher

When John Hamilton asked me to write a foreword to his forthcoming book he said he was in sight of completion of the paintings and well on with the text. He wanted to tell the story of the helicopter in the Falklands Campaign through his paintings, which would not only record the most spectacular moments in the action but also illustrate the vast and complex nature of the logistic support required to sustain the whole operation. His subjects would be units or teams, squadrons or ships, rather than individuals, but individual helicopters would inevitably feature widely. Knowing the depth of his experience and his exceptional talent, and indeed his knowledge of the area, I had no doubt about the outcome and I now write this with the proofs in sight and the satisfaction of seeing that John Hamilton has achieved his aim splendidly.

In this short but intense campaign men and their equipment were tested far beyond normal limits. The men rose heroically to the occasion; and the equipment's performance proved that, properly maintained, it could produce reliability and endurance far in excess of design criteria. Nowhere was this more in evidence than in the helicopters – one example being the eighteen-hour airborne sorties undertaken by Sea Kings from the carriers.

I have spent three-quarters of my working life in the Navy, and most of that time closely involved with the work of the Fleet Air Arm, including one of the first deployments of helicopters to the Falklands and the Antarctic in HMS *Protector*, predecessor of *Endurance*. From 1978 to 1989, however, I was with the Westland Group and this gives me the advantage of a perspective both from the point of view of the operator – it was by no means unusual for me to complain about the performance of our suppliers – and from that of one of the manufacturers most directly responsible for the supply and support of a vitally important piece of equipment. And here it is probably worthwhile mentioning that in peacetime, spares are ordered in the quantities required to support peace-time rates of flying. All very sensible and economical – but during the Falklands Campaign the helicopters were flying in a month more hours than they would normally fly in a year. This demanded a dramatic change of gear by industry to achieve the necessary output, and a logistic support force capable of moving these huge stocks to the scene of action eight thousand miles away.

This operation, which showed once again what our nation can accomplish under pressure, has been fully documented elsewhere, but I am delighted it is so well recorded here.

The Royal Navy has been fortunate to enjoy the support of the Royal Fleet Auxiliary, whose ships have always sailed in close company; today almost all of them operate helicopters. They were never more in demand nor played their part with greater distinction than on this occasion, when they were joined by a large number of merchant ships taken up from trade at exceptionally short notice and whose contribution was outstanding.

Westland has been in the helicopter business for fifty years and is now the repository of all the expertise derived from those who have designed and built rotary wing aircraft in the United Kingdom. The company led the world in adapting the helicopter to operate safely from the busy decks of small ships and, working with the naval staff, has developed a helicopter anti submarine system far in advance of any other. But Westland has not failed to recognise the variety of alternative roles to which this inherently flexible air vehicle can be adapted by design or conversion. The latter nearly always requires complex changes to equipment fitted, and this was a regular feature of Falkland operations. The speed and efficiency with which these changes were effected, usually under appalling conditions, says everything about the skill and dedication of the maintenance crews.

The Falklands Campaign was as much documented, televised and analysed from comfortable armchairs as any other military operation, and this intense interest was maintained throughout. What emerged to the observers at home was a clear demonstration once again of the enduring flexibility of sea power and the new dimension provided by the shipborne helicopter. CORPORATE was essentially a naval operation and the indivisibility of the sea battle on, under and over the sea was crucial. The one serious gap in capability, which became evident only too soon, was the lack of Airborne Early Warning – abandoned with the fixed wing aircraft carriers. The fleet suffered severely, and despite the herculean efforts of the naval staff and the key industrial contractors to equip Sea Kings with a prototype system, which was completed in a record six weeks, they were not in time to take an active part. Nevertheless this work formed the basis of the system now in service with 849 Squadron: the fleet has its 'eyes' again.

All stories are subject to exaggeration, and to that curious superiority about the present that colours our recollections of the past. These splendid paintings will undoubtedly help to keep the record straight and I trust find wide acceptance and acclaim. John Hamilton has been careful to remind us that his Falkland story is about helicopters and that there were many other arms of the three services which contributed to this great team effort. He is, of course, right: the helicopter was only one link in the chain. However, its contribution could not have been provided in any other way; and its many roles were so critical to the success of the whole operation (some two hundred Westland helicopters alone were deployed) that I believe the very special tribute paid in this magnificent book is only too well deserved.

Admiral Sir John Treacher was Director of Westland 1978–89, Vice Chairman 1984–85 and Executive Deputy Chairman 1986–89.

The finishing bay of the Westland factory at Yeovil in Somerset, where nearly all the helicopters in this story were built.

South Georgia.
HMS *Endurance* among the icebergs

On 24 March 1982 the two Wasp helicopters of 829 Naval Air Squadron embarked in HMS *Endurance* took off from the ship's flight deck and headed southeast towards Cumberland Bay on the north coast of South Georgia. HMS *Endurance* is the Royal Navy's warship on station in the South Atlantic. She maintains a British presence in the area and assists the work of the British Antarctic Survey. The helicopters were to land a small observation post to monitor the activities of a group of scrap metal merchants who had landed and raised the Argentine flag on the island, having refused to comply with British immigration formalities.

When it became known that substantial Argentine forces were at sea, heading for the Falkland Islands, *Endurance* was ordered to return to Stanley. Before leaving the area she landed a small detachment of twenty-five Royal Marines at King Edward Point in South Georgia. While on passage she heard of the invasion of the islands and of their surrender, and was ordered to return to South Georgia. By then an Argentine support vessel had landed a company of troops on the island, at the whaling station at Grytviken, and called upon the Royal Marines to surrender. This was followed by the arrival of an Argentine Puma helicopter carrying further reinforcements. On its second trip it was shot down by the marines, who had taken up defensive positions, and a following Alouette helicopter was also damaged. The Argentine corvette *Guerrico* now entered the bay and began shelling the British positions. Waiting until the vessel was well inside and had little room to manœuvre, the marines opened fire with a Carl Gustav rocket, damaging the ship, causing flooding and putting her 3.9 inch gun out of action.

Meanwhile HMS *Endurance* had launched both her helicopters at maximum range to observe the situation. There was no point in prolonging the action against an overwhelming enemy force, so, having obliged the Argentines to use force to occupy the whaling station, the Royal Marines surrendered.

HMS *Endurance* now took up a shadowing role. Being virtually unarmed and painted a conspicuous red, she approached the island at night but remained hidden among the icebergs by day.

HMS Endurance, *the Royal Navy's ice patrol vessel, off South Georgia, from where her aircraft were able to carry out surveillance until the island was recaptured.*

Ascension Island.
Activity on the airfield

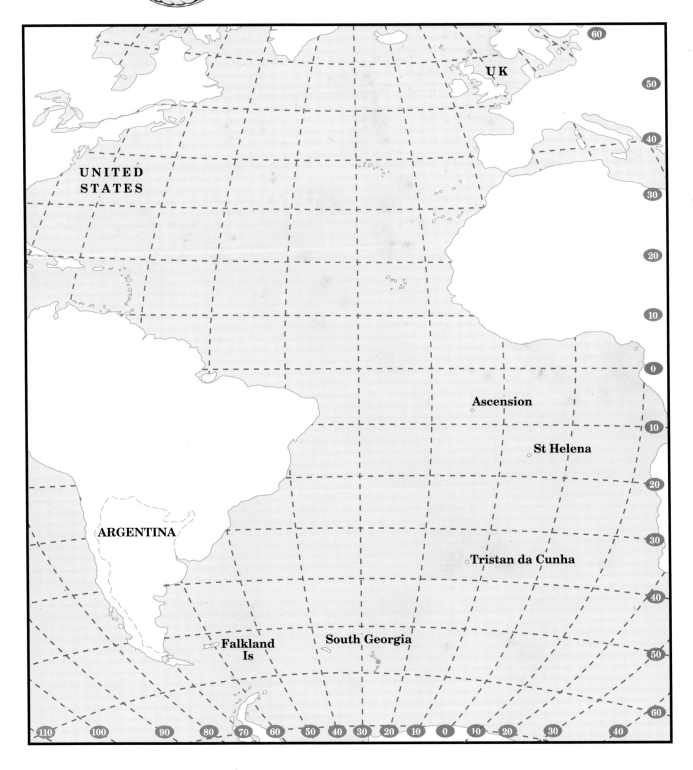

News of the invasion of the Falkland Islands reached London on 2 April, but, because of the worsening situation, plans to dispatch a Task Force had already been made some hours before. It was to be a balanced force, self-sufficient and able to operate for a prolonged period thousands of miles from the nearest base. The Task Force would approach the Falkland Islands only in the event of the Argentine Government not withdrawing in accordance with the United Nations' resolutions, and with world opinion. Nevertheless, it was to be equipped to use whatever force was necessary to make the Argentines leave the islands and adjacent territories in the shortest possible time.

The story which unfolds is the story of all aspects of the helicopter involvement in 'Operation Corporate', the code name for the campaign which followed. Inevitably, and with justification, the story will seem to be one-sided and it will be felt that other units ashore and afloat, forming an integral part of the operations, have been omitted. But this book was never meant to be a history of the campaign, and quite deliberately our story focuses on helicopters.

Naval ships were being loaded with stores in the shortest possible time and, in line with the Government's directives, further support was to come from merchant ships which were requisitioned at short notice. Britain's last conventional aircraft carrier, *Ark Royal*, had been withdrawn from service in 1978, leaving only two other carrier ships operational: the twenty-four year old *Hermes* and the very new *Invincible*. These were listed as anti-submarine warfare (ASW) carriers, and Sea King 5s of 826 and 820 Naval Air Squadrons were allocated to *Hermes* and *Invincible* respectively. Sea King 4s of 846 Squadron, specially adapted for co-operation with the Royal Marines and Special Forces were flown partly to *Hermes* and the remainder allocated elsewhere in the Task Force. Finally, every available space was utilised to accommodate as many Sea Harriers as the decks and hangars would allow. These vertical takeoff aircraft were to protect the Task Force from the whole of the Argentine Air

A Wessex HU5 of 845 Naval Air Squadron at Wideawake airfield on Ascension Island. Thousands of tons of supplies and equipment were airlifted from the UK to the island and distributed by helicopter.

Ascension Island. The arrival of the Task Force

Force and they numbered but twenty-four – with fewer than thirty pilots. In round figures the British Harriers were outnumbered eight to one.

Further helicopter squadrons were earmarked for embarkation. 824 Squadron operated Sea King 2s, as did 825 (formed hastily at Culdrose) and the Wessex Squadrons – 845 with Wessex HU5s and 737 with Wessex 3s – operated flights from various warships and merchant ships in the Task Force, while 847 and 848 were for reinforcements. Among the helicopters flying from Task Force ships as single helicopter detachments were 702 and 815 with Lynxes, 737 with Wessex 3s and 829 with Wasps.

Remarkable as it may seem, HMS *Hermes* and *Invincible*, the assault ship *Fearless*, a number of frigates, and the first echelon of Royal Fleet Auxiliaries (RFAs) sailed on 5 April, just three days after the invasion. They were followed closely by other warships and Royal Fleet Auxiliaries and a number of hastily modified merchant ships.

It happened that a major annual exercise involving twelve warships was taking place off Gibraltar, and the ships themselves were hastily made ready for a passage south. These ships all had helicopters embarked, the older frigates with Wasps and the destroyers with Wessex 3s, but the majority were equipped with Lynx. Two aircraft carriers, three or four submarines, seven destroyers and at least five frigates with support ships were steaming south within three days of the invasion of the Falkland Islands.

The fact that a major part of the fleet had sailed with such speed made it inevitable that a considerable quantity of stores and equipment had not arrived in time to be loaded. The vital link between the UK and the Task Force lay in the British colony of Ascension Island. An outcrop of volcanic rock, it is roughly half-way to the Falkland Islands, but its

importance lay in its 10,000ft runway, built by the United States during World War II. Stationed there normally are oil company representatives, BBC communications staff and cable and wireless and NASA personnel. It is barren and has no indigenous population.

By 4 April five Wessex 5 helicopters had been airlifted by Short Belfast freighter aircraft and work began to accept the continuous flow of stores and equipment which was landed on the island. Within days Wideawake airfield became one of the busiest airports in the world. RAF Transport Command aircraft flew round the clock, supplemented by numerous civilian aircraft on charter. The sheer scale of the logistics problem of administering the airfield from its civilian movements into a huge forward staging area and the speed with which the change was achieved were impressive. The airfield had been administered by Pan American Airways and the co-operation of the civilian population was a major ingredient of success. Within days another dimension developed. As well as a freight and stores staging area, Ascension Island became a support base for the deployment of RAF Nimrod maritime reconnaissance aircraft, and Victor tankers and Vulcan long-range bombers, together with their crews and maintenance staff. As the ships arrived off the island their helicopters were sent ashore, either to ferry out stores forwarded to them, or to form a pool to distribute ammunition and every conceivable item of equipment where it was needed. The fact that the island is an extinct volcano and is covered with larval dust added to the logistical problem: due to dust intake it was impossible to operate helicopters without using the runway, but the dispersal area around the runway was very limited and sufficient space had also to be left for large aircraft to land from the UK and the United States.

This build-up not unnaturally imposed a strain on local resources and for a time water was a problem. Tented accommodation sprang up and working parties were pressed into service, regardless of their trades. Stores arriving from the UK, or by helicop-

ter from ships, were arranged into lanes according to their destination and loaded into cargo nets to await the arrival of the Task Force.

HMS *Hermes* and *Invincible* and their escorts had arrived off the island on 16 April and the next day saw *Fearless*, RFA *Stromness* and five large landing ships anchoring. The carriers had loaded hundreds of tons of stores and equipment needed for other ships or units and these were now ferried ashore by helicopter. For instance *Hermes* transferred two hundred tons of Royal Marines' ammunition, together with C Company of 40 Commando Royal Marines, to the landing ship *Sir Tristram*. On 18 April the two carriers, *Broadsword*, *Glamorgan*, *Yarmouth* and *Alacrity*, together with RFA *Olmeda* and *Resource* sailed south. The combined helicopter force had been engaged in storing their own ships or in general distribution up to the very moment of sailing.

During their few days at Ascension, the Royal Marine Commando Brigade took every opportunity to go ashore to train and to practise quick embarkation and disembarkation from helicopters. This scale of activity meant that aircrews and the helicopter maintenance personnel were stretched to the limit.

As the Task Force headed south with its attendant RFA oilers and stores ships, each with helicopters embarked, a steady stream of civilian ships requisitioned by the Ministry of Defence began to arrive at Ascension. Either they off-loaded or took on thousands of tons of stores, or just picked up a few essential tons which were awaiting them. In each case, it was the helicopter which was responsible for their support as there is no suitable pier or docking facility and only one jetty on the island. The long, continuous and uncomfortable swell forces ships to lie a quarter of a mile offshore. Ascension Island became an indispensable part of the whole Falklands campaign – and the helicopter was an equally indispensable work horse.

Units of the Task Force off Ascension Island on 18 April 1982. An almost continuous stream of helicopters airlifted stores to be distributed among the ships before they sailed south. In the foreground a Sea King 4 of 846 Naval Air Squadron flies past HMS Fearless *with an underslung load.*

RFA *Tidespring* with helicopters airborne off South Georgia

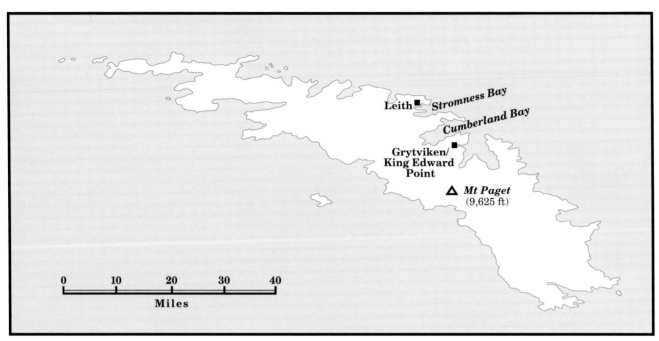

The formal Operation Order for the reoccupation of South Georgia was dropped by Nimrod aircraft to the Task Force Commander (the Commanding Officer of HMS *Antrim*) on 14 April. The opening moves involved the SBS (Special Boat Section, Royal Marines) who would be put ashore from HMS *Endurance* to reconnoitre the Grytviken area while the SAS (Special Air Service) were to 'determine Argentine strength and dispositions in Husvik, Stromness and Leith'. Planning commenced at once. Given reasonable weather there was no reason why a sixteen-man team should not be inserted in daylight by helicopter on top of the Fortuna Glacier, some six miles from the target.

As the Task Force, consisting of HMS *Antrim*, *Plymouth* and *Endurance* and RFA *Tidespring*, approached South Georgia the weather deteriorated into a full gale with hurricane force winds which lasted two days. The weather cleared as they approached the island and at 09.30 on 21 April *Antrim*'s Wessex 3 lifted off to make an essential detailed reconnaissance of the area. The operation seemed possible but the weather was totally unpredictable, varying from relatively clear visibility to total 'whiteout'. From the ships the situation seemed daunting, with rotary turbulence visible high up in the mountains, but by 11.45 *Antrim*'s Wessex 3 was joined by two Wessex 5s from RFA *Tidespring*, loaded with passengers and equipment and together they approached the coast.

The Wessex 3 was the only aircraft fitted with a rudimentary computerised Flight Control System and was the key to the operation. It was essential that the other two Wessex 5s with limited instrumentation kept in visual contact with the ground or the Wessex 3. The route led up from Antarctic Bay in a zigzag between steep mountains on either side. It was considered impossible to fly above the clouds because of icing, and thus vital to maintain visual contact with the ground.

After several attempts to climb the glaciers in thick cloud and turbulence, the three aircraft reached the top of the glacier and landed. The wind speed was between sixty to seventy knots and the

The Royal Fleet Auxiliary tanker Tidespring *in company with* HMS Antrim *off South Georgia. Three Wessex helicopters are airborne preparing to fly the SAS surveillance team to the Fortuna Glacier.*

Rescue from the Fortuna Glacier, South Georgia

pilots had problems keeping the aircraft stationary. The SAS had been landed exactly where they wanted and the three aircraft took advantage of a break in the clouds and returned to the waiting ships. On the glacier the conditions went from bad to worse. Owing to the delay in arriving it was not possible for the SAS to proceed any distance before dark and they dug themselves in as best they could. Hurricane force winds over the glacier sapped the strength of even these highly trained soldiers, and it was impossible to operate in any military context. If they stayed another night in the open, hypothermia

and frostbite would be inevitable. Reluctantly the leader requested evacuation. Meanwhile, on the ship, the wind and sea had made it impossible to stow *Antrim*'s Wessex in its hangar and it remained lashed to the deck. Similarly one Wessex 5 remained on *Tidespring*'s deck. Miraculously the aircraft sustained no damage although they were caked in salt.

The request for evacuation was received at 10.00 on 22 April and a break in the weather at 10.50 enabled the three aircraft to take off. On arrival at the glacier, *Antrim*'s aircraft went up alone while the others waited. The weather clamped down and a raging storm blotted out any visual marks. There was no way through to reach the troops. The aircraft returned to their ships to await a break in the weather. At 13.30 they tried again. This time the

conditions were clearer and they sighted the SAS team, landed and, with the pilots struggling to keep the aircraft stationary on the ground, loaded up. The first Wessex 5 took off just ahead of a squall, hoping to clear the glacier before visibility vanished. With wind speeds of eighty to ninety knots it was overtaken, the pilot could see neither the ground nor the horizon and in the 'whiteout' became disorientated. The aircraft hit the ice and skidded to a halt on its side. No one was seriously hurt. The other two aircraft saw the crash and in minutes had hover-taxied over and embarked the survivors. They took off with the Wessex 3 in the lead, with its electronic equipment scarcely able to cope with 'whiteout' conditions. The Wessex 5 following suddenly lost sight of the leader and lost all bearings. In fact the wind had slewed the aircraft round so that it was flying sideways and a wheel caught in a crevasse and turned it over. This was seen by *Antrim*'s aircraft, but there was no alternative but to return to the ship to disembark passengers and refuel before returning to the scene.

At 16.30 another attempt was made to evacuate in two trips. As *Antrim*'s Wessex 3 (the sole survivor) reached the coast the weather clamped down. Accepting the risk of icing the pilot flew above the clouds but was still boxed in by the mountain sides. The clouds suddenly cleared and they could see the orange day-glo of the life rafts. The situation was critical and it was obvious that it would be impossible to make two trips. Equipment was jettisoned and somehow sixteen bodies and four crew were crammed into the interior. Arms and legs were entangled and stuck out of the door and windows. As it took off the aircraft was a ton over-weight, but the wind assisted the lift. The flight back to *Antrim* was uneventful but it was impossible to hover and gradually to move in to land on the flight deck as too much torque would have to be applied to the gearbox for safety. The aircraft came in on a long descending slide over the port quarter and landed heavily, but without damage. Thus ended a remarkable feat of flying by a thoroughly professional crew, supported by a dedicated and resourceful flight maintenance team.

on the Fortuna Glacier.

The Wessex HAS3 of 737 Naval Air Squadron (Antrim Flight) landing to rescue the SAS troopers and the aircrews of the two crashed helicopters from the Fortuna Glacier.

South Georgia.
Attack on the Argentine submarine *Santa Fé*

With the loss of the two Wessex 5 aircraft there was now an acute shortage of troop lifting capability in the area, and HMS *Brilliant* with her two Lynx helicopters was ordered by Northwood to join *Antrim*. However, military operations had to be postponed because it became clear that the Argentine submarine *Santa Fé* was almost certainly in the vicinity of Cumberland Bay.

The ASW sonar equipment had been removed from *Antrim*'s Wessex some days previously to give more room for troop carrying, and the ship was now seriously at risk from this new threat. The task of installing the equipment is a job which usually takes three days. In the present emergency it was completed in ten hours by *Antrim*'s maintainers and, more important, it worked perfectly at the first test. This considerable achievement was carried out at sea in very bad conditions.

Search areas were allocated and aircraft were launched from all ships during the morning of 25 April. *Antrim*'s Wessex entered Cumberland Bay where a thick fog was reducing visibility to 400 yards. In order to maintain secrecy the helicopter's

radar was not transmitting, but given the weather conditions it was highly unlikely that a visual sighting would be made. Over the last few days the Wessex crew had plotted the position of known icebergs in the area, and a single, one-second radar sweep was made. A longer emission would have alerted the Argentine submarine that it was under surveillance from the air, but this single sweep identified the nine known icebergs. In addition there was one extra blip. More by instinct than anything else, the observer was suspicious and a course was laid to investigate. At a range of half a mile a submarine was sighted on the surface. Approaching from the stern the boat was identified definitely as the *Santa Fé* and depth charges were armed. An extra sweep of the radar enabled the boat's speed to be calculated as 8 knots. The forward throw of a Mark 11 depth charge from a helicopter travelling at 100 knots at 400 feet is 160 yards, so it was calculated that the charges should be released as they passed directly overhead.

As the aircraft flew up the submarine's wake it was seen that the conning tower was unmanned and the periscope was raised. The depth charges were dropped and exploded exactly as predicted. The aircraft was put into a tight turn and two columns of water were seen to rise high above the conning

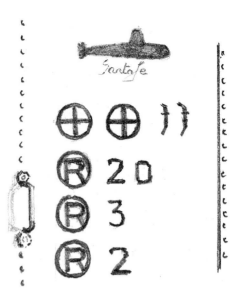

'Battle honours', painted on the fuselage of the Mark 3 Wessex of 737 Squadron (Antrim flight), symbolise the hectic and eventful days off South Georgia and Falkland Sound:

The attack on the Santa Fé
Casualty Evacuation (2) and Special Forces insertions (2)
Rescue of thirteen (later altered to twenty) servicemen on Fortuna Glacier
Rescue of three Special Forces in a Gemini boat off South Georgia
Rescue of two crewmen from a British submarine off South Georgia

tower. The stern rose out of the water and the boat began to steer an erratic course. The Wessex fired its waist-mounted machine gun (GPMG) at the periscope and fin casing, leaving the scene to rearm when *Brilliant*'s Lynx arrived. This aircraft dropped a torpedo to dissuade the submarine from diving, and closed to fire its GPMG. It became apparent that the *Santa Fé* was making for Grytviken in Cumberland Bay.

Helicopters from *Endurance* (which scored a hit on the fin with an AS 12 missile) and from *Plymouth* had by now arrived and shadowed the submarine as it made its way to the jetty and berthed. Diesel oil was seen to be leaking on to the surface of the water and she was down by the stern and listing.

The remaining helicopters were now concentrated on ferrying troops into positions around Grytviken for an assault on Argentine forces. After a spectacular bombardment of nearby rocks, white flags appeared and South Georgia was repossessed without bloodshed.

Disused whaling station Grytviken from King Edward Point.

The Wessex HAS3 of Antrim Flight attacking the Argentine submarine Santa Fé *with depth charges in Cumberland Bay, South Georgia. The submarine was badly damaged but managed to return to Grytviken, where it foundered.*

Ascension Island. Chinook lifting an underslung load

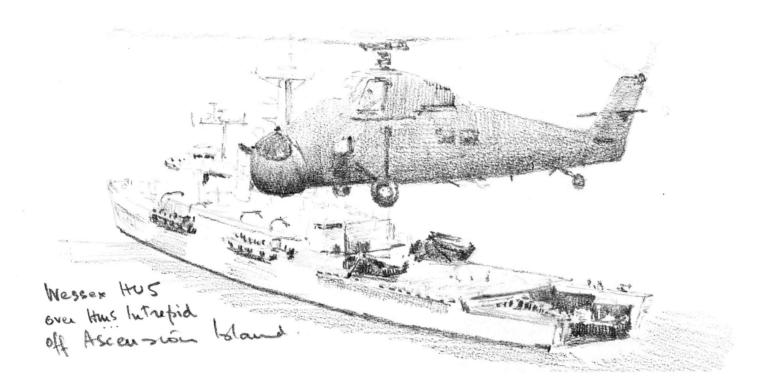

Wessex HU5
over HMS Intrepid
off Ascension Island

Glancing through this book may lead the reader to fail to understand the vitally important role of the Royal Air Force throughout the campaign. With the Task Force carriers the RAF flew Harrier GR3s from No 1 (F) Squadron, flown down from Ascension Island in a marathon flight, but their contribution is beyond the scope of this narrative. No 18 Squadron RAF was equipped with Chinook HC1 helicopters, but only one survived the loss of the *Atlantic Conveyor*, and this aircraft, Bravo November, was to find a special place in the history of the campaign. However it would be grossly unfair, and would produce a completely unbalanced picture, to lose sight of the contribution of the long range transport aircraft of Nos 10, 24, 30, 47 and 70 Squadrons RAF, and of the Vulcan bombing aircraft drawn from Nos 44, 50 and 101 Squadrons.

During the conflict over five thousand people and over six thousand tons of freight were flown by Transport Command to Ascension Island in five hundred sorties. Ground and air defence of the island was the responsibility of the RAF as were maritime patrols by Nimrod MR1 and 2 aircraft. Victor tankers of 55 and 57 Squadrons co-ordinated air refuelling and without them the very long range flights, complicated support flights, and Special Service support facilities, let alone the bombing of Stanley airfield by Vulcans, would have been impossible. These Victor tankers flew over six hundred sorties in complicated and vital operations over extended lines of communication. However, more detailed consideration of the RAF's contribution falls outside our story.

Activity at Wideawake airfield, Ascension Island. A Chinook HC1 of 18 Squadron RAF seen from the cockpit of a Sea King. Green Mountain, with its summit obscured by cloud, is in the distance.

HMS *Arrow* in company with HMS *Hermes*

HMS *Hermes* had recently returned from exercises and was undergoing routine maintenance at Portsmouth when orders were given for her to be brought to forty-eight hours' notice for sea as the situation in the South Atlantic deteriorated. The colossal task of storing and ammunitioning the ship for a long period at sea on active service began and, by working night and day, was completed in time for her to sail on 5 April. Not only had she taken on board her own requirements but also hundreds of tons of stores and equipment for the Royal Marine Commandos and other ships. In addition to her twelve Harriers, two helicopter squadrons were embarked. 826 Naval Air Squadron was an anti-submarine squadron equipped with Sea King 5s, and 846 Naval Air Squadron with Sea King 4s was the Commando support squadron. Modifications to the helicopters were carried out at sea, and after a

very busy few days at Ascension, where stores were distributed and taken on board, the carriers and their escorts sailed south with other units of the Task Force. Intensive flying took place and anti-submarine patrols were flown. In 846 Squadron training in the use of passive night viewing goggles (PNG) was a priority. These image-intensified goggles enabled a pilot literally to see in the dark, but their use required considerable practice and training and there were not many sets available.

Owing to the lack of early warning aircraft the carriers were extremely vulnerable, and picket ships were placed at a distance from them to augment the ASW helicopters and give further early warning of the approach of hostile aircraft and missiles.

On 30 April the thirteen warships and four RFAs of the carrier battle group reached the Total Exclusion Zone (TEZ), an area two hundred miles round the Falkland Islands, and helicopters flew anti-submarine patrols round the clock. A number of false alarms occurred and it was difficult to distinguish a submarine from a whale at times.

HMS Arrow *passes HMS* Hermes *as she moves forward to join the protective screen ahead of the Task Force. 815 Naval Air Squadron's HAS2 Lynx helicopters were embarked in a number of frigates, including HMS* Arrow.

HMS *Hermes*.
Flight deck scene

As stated, intensive training by day and by night took place on the two carriers after leaving Ascension Island. The pace of anti-submarine warfare flying increased with three Sea Kings maintaining a continuous ASW screen up to twelve miles ahead of the carrier group, while a fourth carried out search operations on the surface out to a range of some two hundred miles. An Argentine submarine was thought to be operating to the north of the Falkland Islands and on 1 May three aircraft from 826 Squadron were sent to locate and destroy it. Although it was not located these aircraft refuelled no less than ten times from two frigates, with a crew change in the hover. One aircraft was airborne for ten hours and twenty minutes, the longest period a helicopter had ever remained airborne on an operational mission.

The aircraft embarked in individual ships were no less fully employed, both in surface search duties and in preparation for the landings and for naval gunfire support duties.

Intensive training by day and night was additional to the standing ASW screen round the carrier group. Lynx Wessex and Sea King helicopters are seen operating from the flight deck of HMS Hermes.

Wasp helicopter landing on HMS *Plymouth*

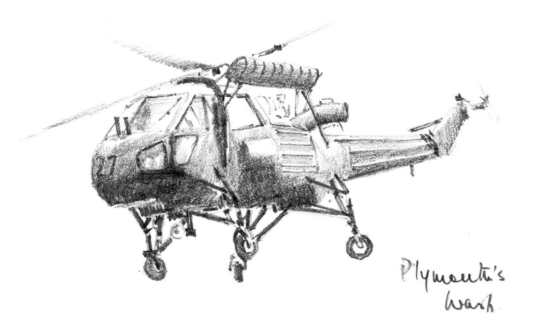

Plymouth's Wasp

829 Naval Air Squadron operated Wasp helicopters from its base at Portland. By 1982 the Wasp had been in service for nearly twenty years and was in the process of being replaced by the Lynx. In fact at the time of the conflict the only frigates deployed in the South Atlantic which operated Wasps were HMS *Active*, *Plymouth* and *Yarmouth*. Each of the survey vessels *Hecla*, *Hydra* and *Herald* (after conversion to hospital ships) carried Wasps, the aircraft being given Red Cross markings with blue anti-collision lights. Finally HMS *Endurance*, the ice patrol vessel, operated two of these aircraft.

The Wasp carries no equipment capable of detecting submarines, but instead it can be armed with two homing torpedoes, depth charges and bombs, and be guided on to a target by its frigate. In addition it can mount two AS–12 wire-guided missiles – the three fired by *Endurance*'s flight damaged the conning tower of the *Santa Fé*. *Endurance*'s flight was fully involved throughout the conflict and made a number of reconnaissance sorties at extreme range.

The flights embarked in the three frigates took part in naval gun support (NGS), evacuation of casualties and in helicopter delivery services (HDS) throughout the campaign. The three survey vessels took on their new and unaccustomed role, and the flights joined the ships' crews for training in all aspects of nursing. From then on they were fully engaged in evacuating casualties and in the delivery of stores to the hospital ship *Uganda*.

In all the squadron's aircraft flew a total of 451 hours, took part in 727 sorties, and made 3,333 deck landings.

A Wasp HAS1 of 829 Naval Air Squadron landing on the flight deck of HMS Plymouth *in rough weather.*

The fight to save HMS *Sheffield*

The two carriers *Hermes* and *Invincible* were absolutely indispensable to the whole campaign. They were floating airfields from which the Harrier jets could operate to strike at the enemy, protect the beach-head and destroy any Argentine aircraft entering the airspace round the Falklands. Thus the Task Force Commander had the problem of keeping his carrier group sufficiently close to the Falklands for his Harriers to fly operationally and for his helicopters to insert reconnaissance parties at night, but far enough away to remain out of range of the Argentine jets based on the mainland.

This is an appropriate moment to stress the effect of the RAF raids on Stanley airfield. While no permanent significant damage was done, yet the runways were denied to the fast jets, and the bombing raids were followed up by Harrier strikes at intervals. It was a crucial factor in the air war, and these remarkable flights with successive in-flight refuelling are far too easily forgotten.

On the morning of 4 May the Task Force was steaming westwards some seventy-five miles south of Stanley. The two vital carriers had their Sea Wolf-armed escorts *Brilliant* and *Broadsword* (see pp. 40–43) as close escort, and in near attendance to the west was an inner ring of three RFA ships. An outer ring consisted of one destroyer and three frigates, and then, on picket station some fifteen to twenty-five miles further west, there were the Type 42 destroyers *Coventry*, *Glasgow* and *Sheffield*.

At 12.15 an Argentine Neptune reconnaissance plane identified the Task Force and within half an hour two Super Étendards had taken off (refuelling from a Hercules tanker aircraft later) and approached their targets, which in fact were the outer screen of the three Type 42s. These aircraft were each armed with one Exocet missile. The Argentine Navy had bought five of these lethal missiles and the Royal Navy was not well equipped to deal with this sea skimming weapon since, in 1982, the Exocet had a clear technological lead. The two aircraft rose to 100ft and made a brief radar sweep which was picked up by HMS *Glasgow* on the outer picket line. She immediately fired chaff and went to action stations, at the same time alerting the Task Force. The aircraft were glimpsed fleetingly on *Glasgow*'s radar for a second as they turned away, having fired their missiles which were streaking towards their targets. One ditched at the end of its run before having found or reached a target, but the other struck HMS *Sheffield*'s starboard side centrally, about six feet above the water line, at seven hundred miles an hour. The 360lb warhead did not explode, which saved many lives, but it entered the ship in the area of the galley, killing eleven men instantly. Ignited by the missile's unspent fuel, fires immediately started, giving off thick black smoke. At the time of the impact the ship's communications system was destroyed so no one knew of the attack. Fortunately a Sea King of 826 Squadron was in the vicinity and lowered her sonar operator to discover the nature of the damage. Within minutes Sea Kings of 846 and 826 Squadron were flown from HMS *Hermes* carrying pumps and other fire-fighting equipment, together with breathing apparatus. HMS *Arrow* and *Yarmouth* came alongside and the fight to save her continued. The injured were flown out from the foc's'le and the flight deck and valiant efforts were made to stem the fires which were raging amidships. As the afternoon wore on it seemed that the battle was being lost and the ship's company was taken off. Efforts were made later to take her in tow, but eventually this proved impossible and the *Sheffield* sank on its way to South Georgia.

The fight to save the Sheffield. *HMS* Yarmouth *and* Arrow *are alongside while aircraft of 826 Naval Air Squadron from HMS* Hermes *assist in ferrying over pumps and evacuating wounded.*

Covert operations at night. Use of passive night goggles

Passive night goggles or PNG were issued to 846 Squadron before they left Portsmouth, but it was 17 April before they had their first chance to evaluate them. From then on training in their use took place at every opportunity. Cumbersome to wear for a pilot who has to have control over all his actions, they give a circular tunnel vision aspect, with everything coloured a sinister yellow green/brown. They also require the cockpit to be blacked out completely. Thus it is only the pilot who can see anything and he must look ahead, the instrument panels being read by the co-pilot. To those flying with him, particularly at low level, it can be an unnerving experience.

From 1 May onwards 846's Sea King 4s were engaged in covert operations to land Special Forces ashore while the carriers were eighty to a hundred and forty miles east of the Falklands. In all, some twenty-five operational sorties were made at night to insert, resupply and recover SAS and SBS reconnaissance parties and to mount offensive raids against enemy positions. On 20 May, for example, four PNG aircraft landed SAS troops in three areas round Darwin and two attempts were made at night to insert Special Forces in the Mount Kent area. Bad weather made this impossible, but the third attempt was successful.

All these PNG tasks were completed without loss, requiring exceptional skill and navigation. In order to avoid enemy radar, low level flying was essential and atrocious weather at times added to the problems.

PNG aircrews were in constant demand, and the fact that aircraft were available at all times illustrates the high standards of maintenance to be found throughout the squadron.

A four-man team from G Squadron SAS kept observation in this outcrop of rock for twenty-six days. They commanded a view from Mount Kent to Stanley and it was from here that they called down an attack on a dispersal area for Argentine helicopters. A pair of GR3 Harriers destroyed one Chinook and two Pumas on 21 May.

The pilot's view through passive night goggles, as he lands at night to pick up a team from the 22nd Special Air Service Regiment which landed on East Falkland ten days before.

Replenishment for HMS *Invincible* from RFA *Fort Austin*

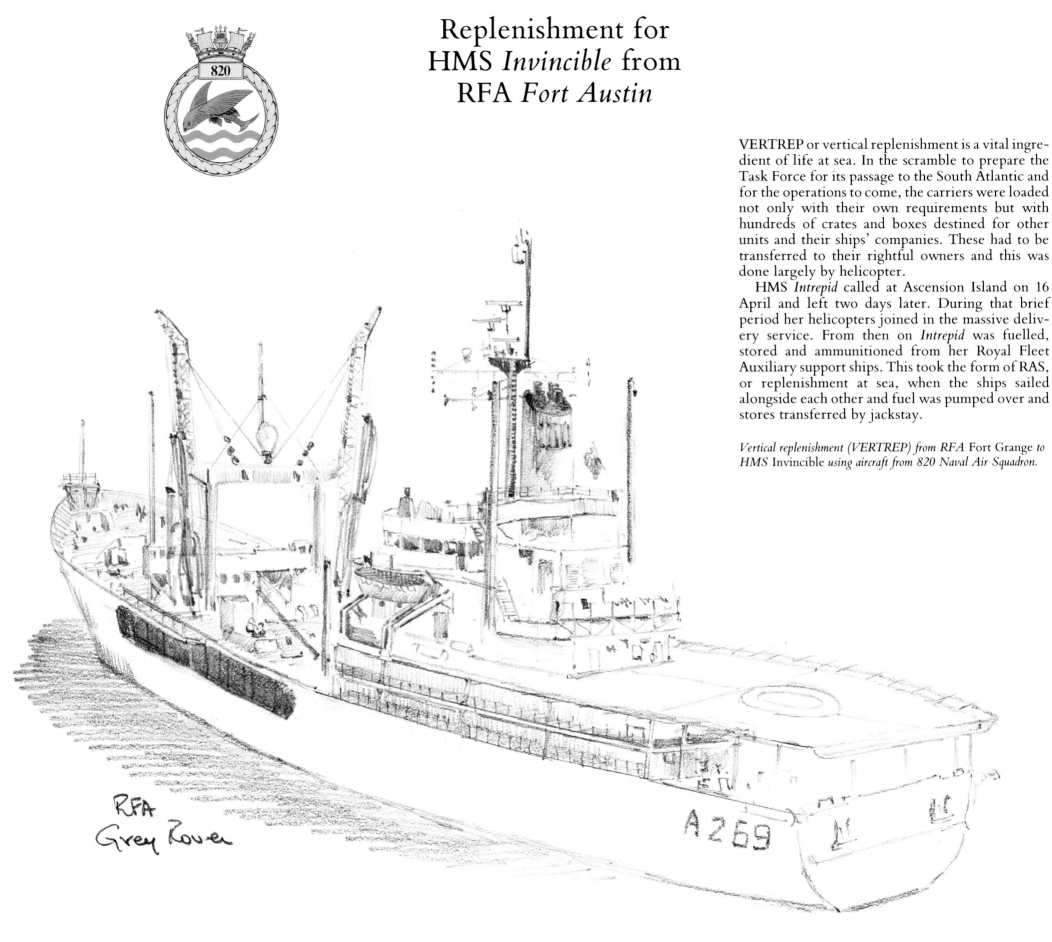

VERTREP or vertical replenishment is a vital ingredient of life at sea. In the scramble to prepare the Task Force for its passage to the South Atlantic and for the operations to come, the carriers were loaded not only with their own requirements but with hundreds of crates and boxes destined for other units and their ships' companies. These had to be transferred to their rightful owners and this was done largely by helicopter.

HMS *Intrepid* called at Ascension Island on 16 April and left two days later. During that brief period her helicopters joined in the massive delivery service. From then on *Intrepid* was fuelled, stored and ammunitioned from her Royal Fleet Auxiliary support ships. This took the form of RAS, or replenishment at sea, when the ships sailed alongside each other and fuel was pumped over and stores transferred by jackstay.

Vertical replenishment (VERTREP) from RFA Fort Grange *to* HMS Invincible *using aircraft from 820 Naval Air Squadron.*

RFA
Grey Rover

A 269

The Pebble Island raid

Pebble Island
5 years after.
May 1987.

SAS reconnaissance teams had been inserted into various parts of the islands to monitor the disposition of Argentine troops. For the most part, Sea King 4s of 846 Squadron were used for these night operations, as troop carriers for the Royal Marines and Special Forces troops. On the night of 11–12 May an eight-man troop from D Squadron 22 SAS Regiment reported details of the existence of a small air base on Pebble Island in West Falkland. Aircraft operating from it included six Pucaras and four T34C Turbo Mentor attack aircraft. These aircraft posed a very real threat to the forthcoming landings and it was essential to destroy them.

On the evening of 14 May HMS *Hermes*, with *Broadsword* as close escort and *Glamorgan* in support, left the rest of the Battle Group and steamed to a position north of West Falkland. At 23.30 two helicopters of 846 Squadron lifted off with forty-five men of D Squadron SAS and a naval gunnery support team. They landed some three miles from the airfield and set off unobserved to the target. The first intimation to the Argentines that all was not well was when explosions rocked the area and the six Pucaras, four Turbo jets and a Skyvan were destroyed. Further explosions lit up the area as stores and fuel dumps were blown up. Finally charges were laid at strategic points in the runway.

As the troops withdrew (with one wounded from Argentine defensive fire), the *Glamorgan* fired ninety rounds of 4.5 inch gunfire, directed by the NGS team. With this covering fire the raiders arrived at the pick-up point without further incident and the helicopters, which had returned to the ship, now arrived back to collect them. It was a thoroughly successful raid and, being the first offensive operation on the Falkland Islands, it was received with acclamation both in the Task Force and at home. For the Argentines it was a double blow. Not only was a strategically important base destroyed, it was also an indication of what was to follow.

The Pebble Island raid. Against a background of exploding delayed charges and gunfire from HMS Glamorgan *offshore, men of D Squadron 22 SAS Regiment are lifted off the island after destroying eleven aircraft on the ground.*

Sea King helicopters approach HMS *Fearless* with underslung loads

Cross decking

Cross decking – distributing stores from a supply ship to HMS Invincible, with HMS Brilliant as close escort.

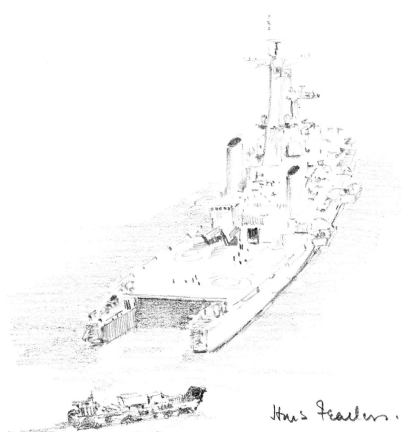

Hms Fearless.

Transfer of stores by helicopter from HMS Hermes to HMS Intrepid as the Task Force heads south.

Goalkeeper.
HMS *Broadsword* with
HMS *Hermes*

The word 'goalkeeper' is synonymous with the two Type 22 frigates HMS *Broadsword* and *Brilliant*, for they formed close escorts to the two carriers *Hermes* and *Invincible*. They were special because they carried the Sea Wolf missile system, the only genuine anti-missile missile in the world, and they were the only ships in the Task Force to be equipped with this system. The Argentines were known to have at least five Exocet missiles. This may not sound much of a threat but each one was extremely dangerous. The Exocet flew at seven hundred miles an hour, had a 360lb warhead, and skimmed over the sea at a height of six to fifteen feet. Conventional anti-aircraft weapons such as the Sea Dart and Sea Slug were not sufficiently effective against wave-top targets, whereas the Sea Wolf could track and destroy even a 4.5 inch shell in flight. So *Broadsword* was tucked in close to *Hermes*, almost as an extension of her own anti-missile defence.

The frigate accommodated a two Lynx flight – the second aircraft having been flown to Ascension Island in a Hercules and reassembled at Wideawake airfield. The aircraft was equipped with radar, torpedoes and depth charges and could carry Sea Skua missiles. The flight was fully occupied on picket duty, naval gunfire support and in the raid on Pebble Island. Following this, one aircraft was slightly damaged by heavy seas and the other by splinters from cannon fire on 21 May. To keep the flight operational another aircraft was borrowed temporarily from *Brilliant*, but this was seriously damaged four days later when a bomb entered the ship and exited through the flight deck. It did not explode, but on its way out it removed the nose of the Lynx positioned on deck. While repairs to the ship were being carried out, the flight managed to repair one aircraft by 1 June, which was used extensively for the duration of the campaign for ESM sorties.

HMS Hermes, *flagship of the Task Force, with her 'goalkeeper' HMS* Broadsword *in the South Atlantic. Equipped with Sea Wolf missile systems she acted as close escort to the carrier.*

HMS *Invincible* with HMS *Brilliant* as close escort

HMS *Brilliant*, a Type 22 frigate and sister ship to *Broadsword*, was the constant companion and 'goalkeeper' to HMS *Invincible*, her Sea Wolf missile system being essential to the defence of the carrier. Before taking up this role, *Brilliant* was detached to make a fast passage south in bad weather to reinforce HMS *Antrim* off South Georgia. With the loss of the two Wessexes on the Fortuna Glacier, her two Lynx helicopters were a valuable addition, particularly in their anti submarine role. Returning to the task force, *Brilliant* became close escort and her helicopters took part in ASW tasks. On 30 April she was detached with the frigate *Yarmouth* and joined by three Sea Kings from 826 Squadron, each aircraft carrying a spare crew. They reached the area thought to contain an Argentine submarine, and the aircraft spent more than ten hours airborne, being refuelled from the decks of the frigates. Nothing was found and eventually *Brilliant* returned to take station close to the carrier.

The following days were eventful for the *Brilliant* flight, and included spotting for naval bombardments of Argentine positions; on 12 May her Sea Wolf systems went into action. In company with HMS *Glasgow*, she was fifteen miles south of Stanley when four Argentine Skyhawks were picked up on radar. *Glasgow*'s Sea Dart system failed, as did her 4.5 inch gun after eight rounds. With the strike little more than a mile away, *Brilliant*'s Sea Wolf system fired three missiles in rapid succession. Two scored direct hits, and the third missile was so violently evaded by the Skyhawk that it crashed into the rough sea. The sequel was not so fortunate, for within twenty minutes a further attack by four more aircraft came in. *Glasgow*'s systems were still being worked on, and the incoming aircraft weaved to such an extent that the Sea Wolf became confused and failed to fire. Both ships had miraculous escapes, *Glasgow* receiving a 1000lb bomb right through the ship without it exploding or causing serious casualties.

During the landings and in the days following, *Brilliant*'s Lynx aircraft were flown throughout daylight hours in support of the ground troops and the build up of stores and equipment, while the ship took on the role of directing the fighters vectored on to the incoming Argentine raids. During one of these the ship was hit by splinters and her missile systems were put out of action for a time.

HMS *Brilliant.*

Brilliant's Lynx with Sea Skua missiles.

HMS Invincible, *the smaller of the two carriers in the Task Force, embarked eight Sea Harrier fighters and the eleven Sea King HAS5s of 820 Squadron. As close escort she has HMS Brilliant, with her Sea Wolf missile system, as she enters the Total Exclusion Zone stretching two hundred miles round the Falkland Islands.*

Dawn landing on Blue Beach, San Carlos

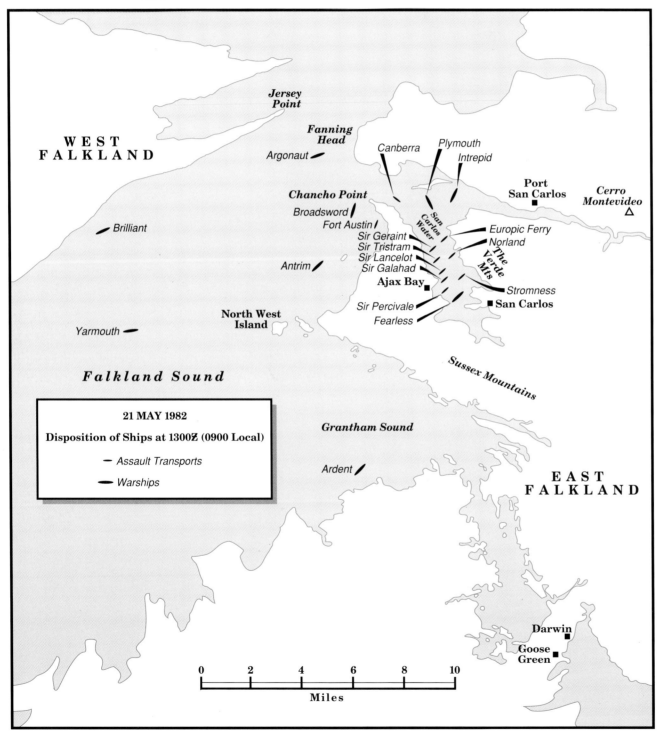

21 MAY 1982

Disposition of Ships at 1300Z (0900 Local)

— Assault Transports

— Warships

As the Task Force entered the TEZ, preparations were made for landing and the ships took station for the final run-in. As will be seen from the map, Fanning Head, an 800ft high bluff, commands the northern entrance to Falkland Sound and an SBS reconnaissance team had ascertained that some fifty enemy gunners and infantry were stationed there. It was essential to remove them before the troop transports entered the sound and anchored.

The Wessex helicopter from HMS *Antrim* flight (737 Squadron) was equipped with a thermal image camera. This shows up living things by forming a 'heat picture' on a TV screen. The helicopter took off from HMS *Antrim* as the ship left the carrier group and headed for Falkland Sound. The position of the enemy heavy weapons company was clearly visible on the screen and the pictures were seen on return to the ship.

This aircraft was now joined by a Wessex from 845 Squadron and together they made three overloaded trips without passive night goggles, landing SBS marines on Fanning Head undetected by the enemy. HMS *Antrim* then fired 268 4.5 inch shells in thirty minutes into the Argentine positions and the marines captured those who survived. The entrance to Falkland Sound was now secured without loss to the Task Force.

To the south a force of SAS from D Squadron had been airlifted by 846 Squadron and a devastating attack made on the Argentine positions at Goose Green. So fierce was the attack that the enemy reported that it was in battalion strength.

Before dawn on 21 May the landing went ahead, not without some delay and confusion, but mercifully without opposition and finally with complete success. 2 Para and 40 Commando were the first ashore at Blue Beach, the former moving south to deny the Sussex mountains to the Argentines. This was followed by 45 Commando who went ashore on the opposite side of San Carlos at Ajax Bay; and finally, at Port San Carlos in the north, 3 Para completed the defence of San Carlos Water.

As soon as the beach-heads were secure the troopships entered and anchored. The first priority against the expected air attacks was to airlift the

Dawn landing at Blue Beach, San Carlos. A helicopter from 845 Naval Air Squadron, embarked in RFA Resource, *bringing ashore an underslung load of mortar ammunition.*

Sea King helicopter delivering ammunition to 42 Commando

AA Rapier Battery ashore. By nightfall all twelve sites were occupied (though not operational), but two Gazelle helicopters of 3 CBAS were hit by small arms fire and crashed. Despite an arduous day's flying by every available helicopter, and the non-stop ferrying of stores in landing craft and mexifloats, unloading was still behind schedule.

It was not long before air strikes added to the problems of a worrying day. Helicopters dodged incoming Argentine aircraft by flying low, but the defensive barrage made any movement extremely dangerous. At the end of the day thirteen Argentine aircraft had been destroyed without the loss of a single Harrier. However, one British warship had been lost and four damaged. Attrition at this rate would bring disaster to the British forces, but fortunately the air losses suffered by the Argentines resulted in their decision to abandon mass air attacks. The superior combat air patrols flown by *Hermes* and *Invincible* and the layered anti-air defence of the warships were the deciding factors.

The air attacks on 21 May were concentrated mainly on the protecting warships in Falkland Sound. The carriers had had to stay some 130–150 miles from the beach-head because of the danger of Exocet missiles and other air attacks, and that meant that continuous air cover could not be given by the Harriers. HMS *Antrim* was controlling them from a central position and was able to give details of raids in progress, but the proximity of land and the very low level approach precluded any early air raid warning. Until the Rapier batteries became operational the defence of the beach-head rested mainly on the warships, further hampered by the scattered nature of the anchorage; but there were also problems for the Argentines. Low level high speed approach with hills surrounding the targets gave only seconds for the release of the bombs, which then had scant time in which to become armed before reaching their targets. Nonetheless they achieved considerable success. At the end of the first day *Argonaut* was out of action, *Ardent* was sinking and *Brilliant, Antrim* and *Broadsword* had been slightly damaged. However, none of the amphibious or merchant ships had been hit. During this time over three thousand troops and a thousand tons of ammunition and stores had been landed. The helicopters had flown continuously, only taking cover at the moment of an Argentine raid. Nonetheless, unless further measures were taken, the following day could see even more serious losses. Thus HMS *Coventry* and *Broadsword* (with a combination of Sea Dart and Sea Wolf missiles systems) were placed as a 'missile trap' in the open sea to the north of Falkland Sound. They were vulnerable but effective over the next few days, so much so that a special enemy co-ordinated air strike was directed against them and the carrier group on the Argentine National Day – 25 May.

The attack by four Skyhawks made towards *Broadsword* first and one bomb hit her stern without exploding. At a crucial moment in the next strike, *Coventry*'s manoeuvres placed her between *Broadsword*'s Sea Wolf system and the targets. No missiles were fired and *Coventry* was hit; she was soon in a sinking condition. Within minutes helicopters from 846 and 826 Squadrons were scrambled from the carriers and the rescue began. Although nineteen men had been killed in the explosion, the casualties could have been much higher. As the ship began to heel over and sink the ship's company were winched from the deck, from the sea and from life rafts. Some were picked up by *Broadsword*.

A CPO aircrewman from 846 was lowered down to a raft to assist in winching up the occupants. From there he swam from raft to raft, guiding rescuers and encouraging survivors.

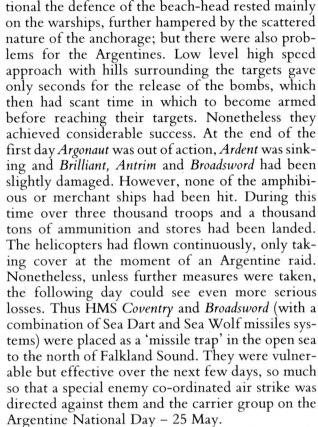

Marines of 42 Commando dig in above the beach at San Carlos, while a Sea King HC4 of 846 Naval Air Squadron brings in a load of ammunition.

Searching for survivors from HMS *Coventry*

HMS Coventry
Memorial
Pebble Island
AS 87

Within thirty minutes of the attack on *Broadsword* and *Coventry* the carrier group itself was under attack. Helicopters were winching *Coventry*'s survivors from the water as two Super Étendards, refuelled from a Hercules tanker, attacked from the north. Exocets in flight had been detected by *Ambuscade*, and chaff rockets were fired. The missiles veered away, seeking a target which was not protected by chaff. The two carriers were surrounded by a ring of supply and warships and most of the former did not carry this defensive device. The largest was *Atlantic Conveyor*. Her role was that of aircraft 'carrier', in that she transported aircraft and was able to fly off vertical take-off Harriers and helicopters. She carried fourteen Harriers. Mercifully for the Task Force these aircraft had been flown off to the carriers. However, her upper decks were still full of helicopters and below decks were thousands of tons of stores, including tentage for nearly ten thousand troops, steel runways, vehicles and the capability to be a major helicopter repair ship. She was to have been detached from the carrier group within the hour to proceed to Falkland Sound and anchor that night. As it was, one Wessex and one Chinook had been flown off to assist in moving stores round the group. It was at that moment that one or two Exocets struck with devastating effect. When the attack had been detected, the ship immediately began to turn to present as small a profile as possible to the oncoming missile, but it struck her on the port side, running up the inside of the vessel causing fierce fires. Within seconds the ship was engulfed in acrid smoke. Explosions followed and it was impossible to control the fires. Despite a gallant attempt to save her, the fires were in danger of reaching the two hundred tons of bombs she carried and half an hour after the attack the order to abandon ship was given. Dusk was falling and there was a cold swell as helicopters took off some members of the ship's company from the bow, but the majority climbed down into the life rafts off the stern and were picked up by the frigates standing by.

Searching for survivors from HMS Coventry, hit by an Exocet missile. As the destroyer began to heel over, the ship's company took to the life rafts. Some were picked up by HMS Broadsword, and a stream of helicopters winched the remainder out of the rafts.

I visited the memorial on the fifth anniversary of the sinking of HMS Coventry. *It was a cold day, and strong winds blew sheets of rain across the grey-green hillside as my army sergeant companion and I climbed to the highest point of the island. Looking up I could see the cross silhouetted against the dark sky, but what I couldn't understand was why there were tiny red specks clinging to the heather. I picked one up and found that it was a little piece of bright red cloth, and as I climbed higher these little red dots became more numerous. Stopping for a moment to get my breath back, I looked up. What I saw was a red carpet which came to a point like an arrowhead at the summit. As I neared the memorial the reason became plain: these were thousands of little pieces of British Legion poppies, blown by the wind, but caught in the heather.*

All round the base of the monument were wreaths and bunches of flowers – and dozens of ships' crests. It seemed as though every ship and every unit was represented there. Everything was held down by heavy stones, and carpeting the area, caught in the heather, were these masses of tiny red poppy petals. It was a very moving moment for both of us. As I was sitting doing my drawing a helicopter approached and hovered over the memorial, as if in salute, and then flew away, the noise of its engines remaining with me as I finished the sketch.

SS *Atlantic Conveyor* at sea flying off a Chinook helicopter

Without doubt the loss of the *Atlantic Conveyor* was the single most damaging setback to the whole campaign. Helicopter lifting capacity was the lynch pin of the whole operation and the loss of the three Chinooks was particularly serious but, taken with the further loss of five Wessex and the repair facilities, it now became acute. This loss prevented 3 Commando Brigade from being 'air portable'. Not only would the majority of the two brigades have to walk, but there would be insufficient lift to carry all the guns *and* ammunition, together with the fuel and rations. With the onset of winter, the loss of the tented camp would add considerably to the discomfort of troops and prisoners alike.

Despite the lack of spares, however, the one surviving Chinook, codenamed 'Bravo November' was destined to play a distinguished role in the closing stages of the campaign (see p. 74).

SS Atlantic Conveyor (Cunard Line), a roll on–roll off ship, was in company with the carriers when an attack by Argentine aircraft was launched. An Exocet missile heading for the carriers was deflected by chaff and veered towards Atlantic Conveyor, *which it hit, causing uncontrollable fires. Her cargo of eight helicopters, including three Chinooks, and thousands of tons of valuable stores were lost with the ship.*

Flying off the
Harriers – ss Atlantic Conveyor

Sea King in AEW role

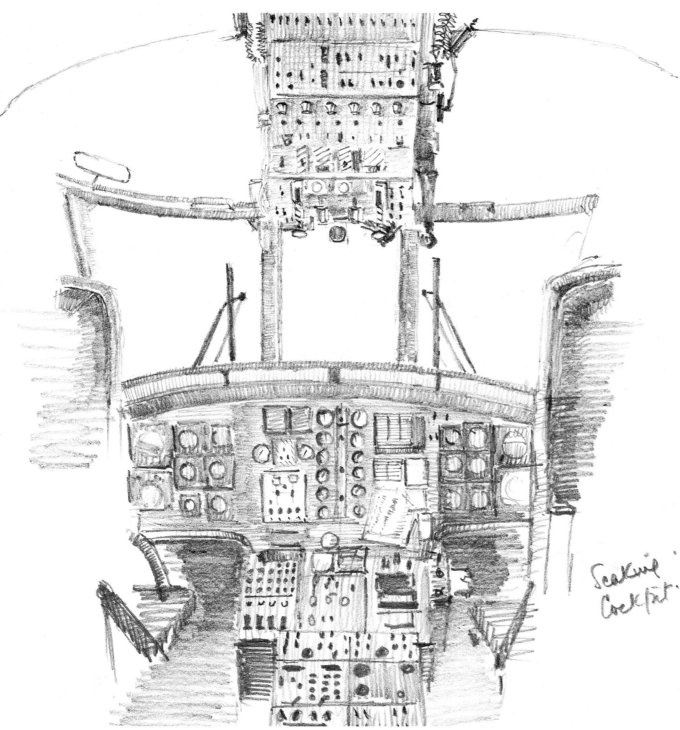

Seaking Cockpit.

Strictly speaking this painting should not figure in our story, for the aircraft took no part in the campaign. It has been included because of the critically important role it now performs.

The Royal Navy had been without its own Airborne Early Warning cover (AEW) since the Fairey Gannet was taken out of service in 1978. It was vital that the Task Force, which was operating 8,000 miles from the UK, should have its own 'local' AEW cover. The Argentine Super Étendards with their Exocet missiles could have been tracked from the coast of Argentina and Harriers targeted to intercept them if an early warning aircraft had been airborne. In the same way the air raids on the ships in Falkland Sound could have been broken up before they reached their targets had the Royal Navy had the facilities to detect their approach.

As it was, under pressure of operational necessity the Searchwater radar fitted to the Nimrod aircraft was available, as was the Thorn–EMI variant, modified to allow it to detect aircraft. By working night and day Westlands of Yeovil fitted this new development to a Sea King, starting work only a week after a feasibility study had been completed. The new radar aerial was fitted to the starboard side of the fuselage on a swivelling arm, and by 14 June (the day of the surrender) the new AEW radar was ready for acceptance trials, being cleared for service entry on 30 July. On 2 August two aircraft were flown to HMS *Illustrious* as she passed down the English Channel en route to the South Atlantic.

It shows just what can be achieved under pressure, but without doubt the need for AEW cover was one of the most crucial lessons learned from the Falklands conflict. One has only to consider the effect of the Exocet attack on *Atlantic Conveyor*. The presence of the Argentine Super Étendard was only known to the carrier group literally seconds before the missile struck.

The airborne early warning carried by this Sea King AEW2 of 824 Naval Air Squadron is not strictly a part of this story for it arrived after the Argentine surrender. It is included because one of the most forceful lessons learned from the campaign was the need for adequate early warning of the presence of hostile aircraft.

Sonar screen

There was an important difference in the ways in which the Royal Navy and the United States Navy viewed the role of the anti submarine warfare (ASW) helicopter. The Royal Navy gave the aircraft the necessary equipment to allow it to operate tactically quite independently of its parent carrier, so that the tactical centre was on board the helicopter and not the carrier. In the United States' view the ship was in tactical command and directed the helicopter which was to be used in finding the exact location and then destroying the submarine. As the submarine's capabilities improved over time – it was developed to travel faster and more quietly, and to dive deeper with more effective weapons – so the technology had to keep pace to detect and destroy it. The Wessex did not have the range for the future, so Westlands developed the Sea King (under licence agreement with Sikorsky of America). The programme development undertaken by Westlands was sufficiently successful for the Royal Navy to decide to re-equip with the anglicised version of the original American design. As a result this aircraft was to become the most potent and effective hunter/killer in the world.

The most obvious distinguishing feature of the Mark 5 Sea King is the large dorsal radome on the top of the aircraft fuselage. Housed inside the dome is the antenna for the new Sea Search radar, which has nearly doubled its original range. On the seventeen-inch radar screen it can be set in three different modes. In the first the helicopter itself appears at the centre of the screen, stationary in relation to its surroundings; in the second the aircraft seems to be moving over a stationary sea or land; and in the third the helicopter's own position can be offset from the centre of the display. All this can be achieved whatever the interference normally cluttering up the radar screen in bad weather.

Alongside this, and equally important, is the Lightweight Acoustic Processing and Display System. The sonar buoys are lowered into the water while the aircraft hover at forty feet over the sea, and the data received from these buoys is interpreted on a printout chart in detail. This is handled by the sonar operator, usually up to the rank of Chief Petty Officer, who sits beside the observer. During operations it is the observer who is in tactical command of the aircraft, which he controls from the rear cabin situated in the body of the helicopter. It is in fact a mini operations room carried on an airborne platform, for the Sea King in its ASW role is comparable to a frigate in its operational effectiveness. It has a manoeuvrability and speed far greater than any ship, and yet it can carry an impressive array of armaments, fully equipped to destroy any submarine after making an initial contact. During the campaign these weapons were a combination of up to four homing torpedoes and/or depth charges, in addition to machine guns mounted in the fuselage.

Two more systems are incorporated into the Mark 5, one being the Decca navigational system which tells the aircrew where they are in relation to latitude and longitude, what course to steer to reach the next desired point, and when that point has been reached. The other new piece of equipment is the Magnetic Anomaly Detector (MAD), which tells the observer whether the suspicious object is made of metal, or whether after all it is only an innocent whale.

This is a very brief and sketchy outline of the detection electronics carried aboard the two Mark 5 squadrons – 826 Naval Air Squadron embarked in HMS *Hermes* and 820 in *Invincible* – in their anti submarine role. Both the carriers were extremely vulnerable since their operational roles required them to remain as close to land operations as possible to enable the Harriers to give protection and support to the ground forces. The threat of submarine attack was very real, for Argentina had a modern ex-German submarine, the *San Luis*, which was known to be operating off the Falkland Islands. Their other operational boat, the *Santa Fé*, had been put out of action by depth charges and SS12 attacks by *Antrim* and *Endurance*'s flights off South Georgia but, until the *San Luis* could be sunk or removed from the area, a continuous ASW screen had to be mounted. Helicopters were positioned some twelve miles ahead and on the flanks of the carrier group in the hover with their sonar buoys lowered into the water. After nine minutes they would leapfrog forward about two miles, forming their protective screen.

As the task force headed south from Ascension Island, the Mark 5s began their continuous task of searching for Argentine submarines and generally protecting the carriers. As they approached the Falkland Islands their role was extended to enforce the blockade within the two hundred mile Total Exclusion Zone. Throughout this period three aircraft were airborne at all times, forming the screen, and the strain on aircrew and maintainers alike was intense, for total and prolonged concentration was required during each sortie, flown in all weathers by day or night and sometimes with huge seas running. Aircraft availability rates were maintained at between 75 and 85 per cent which, when compared with peace-time figures of about 60 per cent, speak for themselves. During the conflict 820 Squadron flew 2,150 hours on nearly 700 ASW sorties, and nearly as many on other types of operations, while 826 flew more than 3,000 hours. Although no Argentine submarines were detected or attacked, the commanding officer of the *San Luis* has reported that his boat was harried by ASW helicopters for more than twenty hours during one patrol.

The rear cabin of an ASW Sea King 5 of 820 Squadron. The Observer is in overall tactical command of the helicopter during operations and he controls it from here in the body of the aircraft. The sonar operator is sitting to his right.

A Mark 5 Sea King engine has been opened up for routine inspection on board HMS Invincible.

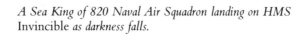

A Sea King of 820 Naval Air Squadron landing on HMS Invincible *as darkness falls.*

Unloading at Ajax Bay

Ajax Bay opposite San Carlos and on the west bank of San Carlos Water is bleak, but there is a good beach, well protected with a flat area behind. The old disused refrigeration plant was some hundred and fifty yards inland and this large building became the Field Hospital. The area round it was suitable for the speedy handling of all kinds of stores – fuel, ammunition, rations and hundreds of tons of miscellaneous equipment. Forklifts could operate on the hard surface and trucks could be driven down the landing craft ramps. Within hours a large staging area was being laid out. Helicopters landed outside the refrigeration plant and also on a pad some two hundred yards to the north. 3 Commando Brigade is unique in the British Army in that it has its own Logistics Regiment. They are fully trained marines but divided into medical, transport workshops, ordnance and a headquarters. They were based at Ajax Bay and their task was the immediate off-loading and stacking ashore in order of priority of the thousands of different items, followed by speedy distribution to the units. The build-up continued and soon thousands of green ammunition cases, boxes of rations and hundreds of drums of oil and diesel were covering a larger and larger area.

Unloading stores at Ajax Bay by landing craft, mexifloat and helicopter. This area opposite San Carlos was the central stores and ammunition depot for the ground forces.

Casualty evacuation from near Darwin Hill, Goose Green

Although the Argentine planners had expected British Forces to land in the vicinity of Stanley, the 12th Regiment of Infantry, together with one company of the 25th Regiment, were now in defensive positions in the Darwin and Goose Green areas (where the largest settlements were located). D Squadron 22 SAS Regiment had been in action as a diversion during the initial landings, yet the Argentines had not been removed and thus posed a considerable threat to the Commando Brigade's beach-head and to the campaign as a whole. The 2nd Bn The Parachute Regiment was ordered to attack and capture the positions on 27–28 May. Helicopter support was to be given by 846 Squadron of Sea King 4s to airlift three 105mm guns of 8 Battery 29 Commando Regiment RA with their ammunition. 3 Commando Brigade Air Squadron (3 CBAS) provided two Gazelles and two Scouts whose initial task was to ferry ammunition forward to the advancing companies.

The main Argentine defensive position was on the forward slope of a small rise known later as Darwin Hill. The ground there is completely devoid of cover and the enemy had mined some of the approaches, with 105mm guns in support and AA guns in a ground defence role. Finally, they could call on air strikes from Stanley. It was a secure defensive position and held more troops than the British force.

Preparations were complete on 27 May and the battalion marched the eight miles to the start line forward of Camilla Creek House. The 105mm guns had been brought up and HMS *Arrow* was stationed off shore to give further gunfire support. Owing to her exposed position, the ship would have to be withdrawn at first light. In the event this was to have considerable significance, as the Paras only came up against the main defensive position, stretching from Boca House to Darwin Hill, as it was getting light. There was no cover and three companies were heavily committed with the danger of the momentum of the attack faltering. The Commanding Officer came forward and, after a further push forward which attracted casualties, he and three others charged the position. All were killed but the dash of this attack, in full view of his men, launched a final attack which overran the enemy and white flags were seen. Without stopping the Paras moved on and captured the airfield. By nightfall those of the enemy who had not surrendered were squeezed into the Goose Green area and within hours it was all over.

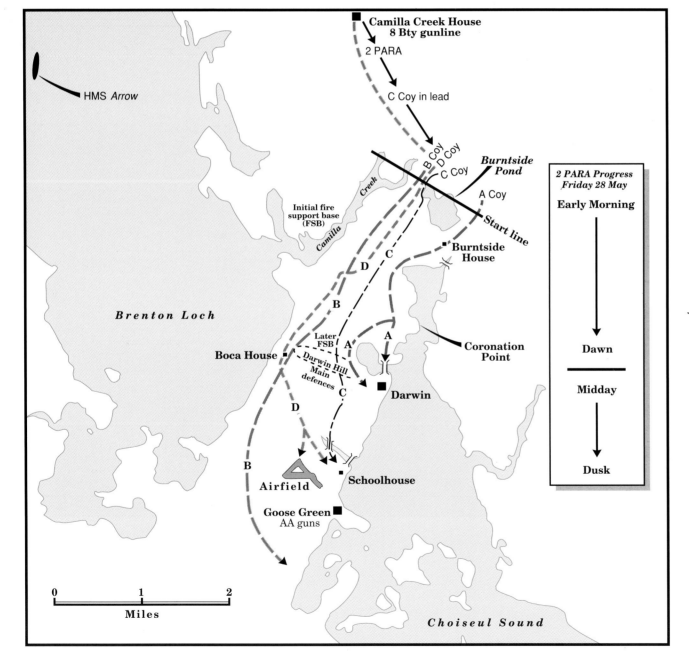

A Scout AH1 of 3 Commando Brigade Air Squadron (3 CBAS) landing near Darwin Hill to evacuate wounded during the battle for Goose Green. Gorse has been set alight by tracer bullets during the night.

Commando Brigade Air Squadron maintenance area at San Carlos

Throughout the battle the CBAS helicopters were used to bring up ammunition and evacuate casualties, many of whom were airlifted from the battlefield direct to the field hospital. Pucara aircraft attacked the Scouts, and in one action two Scouts were attacked by two Pucaras while on their way to evacuate wounded. The first attack was evaded and one Pucara made a second attack. In one Scout the observer was hit in the foot, but the pilot was killed instantly. The aircraft crashed but the observer was thrown clear and, though badly wounded, was picked up and taken to Ajax Bay. At this point two Scouts from 656 Squadron Army Air Corps (AAC) were ordered to assist in casualty evacuation (CASEVAC) and this went on all day, the aircraft bringing up ammunition as they returned to the battle.

The Commando Brigade differs from other formations in that it has its own air squadron – 3 CBAS, equipped with nine Gazelles and six Scout helicopters. 5 Infantry Brigade also had light aircraft, and 656 Squadron Army Air Corps was under their command. They were equipped with six Gazelles and three Scouts but before the brigade arrived, the three Scouts were attached to 3 CBAS. All the aircraft in these two squadrons operated in direct support of the ground forces.

Before daybreak on 21 May all the aircraft had taken off from the landing ships that had brought them south and were supporting the landings. Two Gazelles supported the SBS attack on Fanning Head and two took on the difficult task of confirming that there was no enemy presence on or near sites earmarked as Rapier sites. These were mainly in areas that ground forces would only be able to reach with difficulty and troops would therefore be inserted by helicopter later in the day. The aircraft each had a GPMG in the rear port doorway for protection, but it was not an easy task.

During the day the squadron's Gazelles escorted Sea Kings delivering ammunition and stores and in error one of these aircraft overflew the leading troops. Realising his mistake the pilot turned back but the escorting Gazelle was hit and crashed. The pilot died of his wounds. A second Gazelle was shot down by the same Argentine unit in similar circumstances a short while later and both air crew were killed. During that first day ashore three of the squadron's Scouts were actually airborne for more than eight hours.

The squadron was now based ashore at San Carlos and the aircraft were dispersed among the shearing sheds of the farm, the aircrew and maintainers sleeping in the sheds. The aircraft were in constant demand, supporting the Commando Brigade as they moved forward towards Stanley.

Back at San Carlos the maintainers worked all hours to keep the aircraft flying, and it is a measure of their professionalism and expertise that these light helicopters were kept flying, often in atrocious conditions of snow, wind and rain, and that no tasks were turned down due to lack of maintenance.

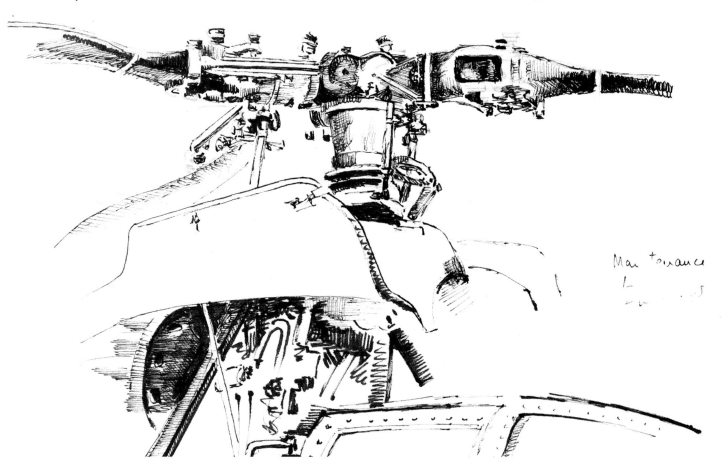

Aircraft of 3 CBAS operated ashore from San Carlos as soon as troops landed. Here they are seen in their maintenance area among the shearing sheds of the settlement.

View from the cockpit of a Gazelle helicopter over East Falkland

3 Commando Brigade relied almost entirely on air lift for support during its move forward in the following weeks. Valuable as they were, the Scouts and Gazelles of 3 CBAS and 656 Squadron AAC were not designed for heavy lift loads and were more suitable for smaller individual sorties not requiring larger aircraft. The sinking of the *Atlantic Conveyor* meant that there were no more helicopters coming forward as reinforcements and extra lift capability in the immediate future, except for the one Chinook; and although this did valuable service it was not enough. Out of one squadron's eleven Sea Kings, one was permanently allocated to the Rapier Battery sites for fuel and the four machines equipped with PNG were not normally available during the daytime, due to the strain of night flying, and maintenance. The remaining six Sea Kings and nine Sea King 2s of 825 Squadron, together with five Wessex 5s, were all that were available for all troop, equipment and logistic movement ashore for the whole brigade. This included guns *and* ammunition, but more seriously it also included the ferrying tasks from the ships at anchor to the shore. Thus any thought of airlifting 42 Commando to Teal Inlet with the required build-up of equipment was out of the question.

The shortage of helicopters was not the only problem. The situation was compounded by the bad weather, which meant that it had taken five nights to fly D Squadron SAS to the Mount Kent area. However, it was thought possible to airlift one company of 42 Commando, the mortar troop and three light guns to consolidate this vital position which overlooked the whole area towards Stanley. Just after the first aircraft took off at night, a full blizzard blotted everything out and the helicopter was forced to return, bucking and lurching dangerously in the darkness.

On 27 May, 45 Commando and 3 Para had been forced to march from Port San Carlos, first to New House, then to Douglas Settlement and finally to Teal Inlet. The ground was boggy and there were tussocks of grass that made ankles particularly vulnerable to sprains. Since this march coincided with the battle for Goose Green, helicopters were not available to airlift the bergens (packs), so the marines and paratroopers carried them. Fighting order with ammunition weighed approximately seventy-six pounds, and with the rucksack it was about a hundred and twenty pounds. The crushing weight of this burden tried even the toughest troops. Marching in darkness was worse than in daylight, but the marines reached the first planned stop at New House at 22.00. To add to the misery it rained heavily and sleeping bags were soaked. Douglas Settlement was reached next day, the men moving in fighting order only, but on arrival at Teal Inlet they found that the enemy had vacated the area two days before.

The men of 3 Para who had made the same back- and ankle-breaking march had taken the rather more direct route to Teal Inlet via the Anoyo Pedro river. Both columns had expected to have to fight at the end of the march and it was a tremendous relief to find the enemy gone.

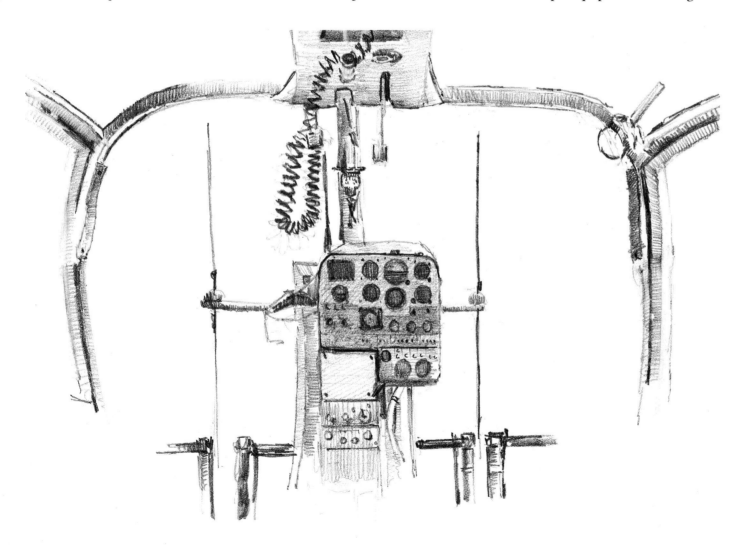

View from a Gazelle AH1 during the 'yomp' from San Carlos to Teal Inlet.

The Field Hospital at Ajax Bay, with a Sea King taking off

Ajax Bay Bomb damage

Ajax Bay.

One of the more remarkable achievements to come out of the Falklands campaign was the speed with which casualties were airlifted direct to the Forward Field Hospital housed in a disused meat refrigeration plant at Ajax Bay. Nicknamed 'The Red and Green Life Machine', after the red and green berets of the Paras and Commandos, it was a self-contained part of 3 Commando Brigade Logistics Regiment with its own surgical teams.

The original plan had been for casualties to be evacuated direct to SS *Canberra* before further evacuation to the hospital ship *Uganda*, at sea to the north of the islands. All this changed when the Argentine airforce struck at Falkland Sound on D-Day. As a result of the air attacks the *Canberra* was ordered out of the area as the risk of her loss was too great. This change of plan meant the immediate transfer ashore of the Field Hospital. The refrigeration plant at Ajax Bay was the obvious choice and it was operational the next day. From then on, and for the next twenty days, over six hundred battle casualties were treated there. It is not only a measure of the surgeons' skill that so many lives were saved – and no one who entered Ajax Bay as a casualty was lost – but equally the result of the allocation of helicopters for immediate CASEVAC missions, and the speed with which these were flown from the forward areas. On 27 May forty-seven operations were performed after the Battle of Goose Green. On the same day two enemy unexploded bombs landed a few feet away from the operating tables; work went on as usual. A further air raid detonated some ammunition and this continued to explode at intervals for some time. Part of the plant was demolished, but fortunately it was the area furthest away from the hospital wards.

All types of helicopter were used for casualty evacuation, and it became standard practice for those carrying wounded to approach the landing pad with their lights on.

The Field Hospital in the disused refrigeration plant at Ajax Bay. Helicopters brought wounded from the battlefield or ships at sea direct to the hospital, from where they were flown out to SS Uganda offshore.

Sea King approaching
SS *Uganda*

HMS Herald's Wasp.

HMS HECLA.

SS *Uganda* was in the Mediterranean on her normal educational cruise, carrying over one thousand school children, when she was requisitioned on 11 April. She reached Naples two days later, disembarked her passengers and sailed again for Gibraltar dockyard. Sixty-five hours after her arrival she sailed again (on 19 April), but this time she was painted white with red crosses and transformed into a hospital ship with nearly eleven hundred beds. A helicopter pad had been fitted aft and operating theatres, recovery rooms, high and low dependency wards, intensive care facilities and all the specialist functions and needs for a major floating hospital were provided. It is a truly remarkable story of co-operation, clear thinking and decision-making that enabled the ship to be fully staffed with a 135-strong medical team, stored and provisioned by the time she left Ascension. Stores included a two hundred and fifty bed portable and packaged hospital and ninety tons of medical supplies which had been flown in from the UK. Fresh water was a problem as the ship was unable to process it herself, but later HMS *Intrepid* transferred two reverse osmosis generators and 6,182 tons of water (out of a total of 10,750) were made in this way.

Uganda arrived just north of the Falklands on 11 May, in time to take on the first casualties – from HMS *Sheffield*. As the days passed she moved steadily nearer to Ajax Bay, and at the peak of her work she received 159 casualties in four hours, with the helicopters stacked up waiting their turn to land. Normally she would receive forty to seventy casualties per day, from both sides. Once they were fit to travel the wounded were transferred to the smaller ships *Hecla*, *Hydra* and *Herald* for transfer to Montevideo and then by air to the UK. These survey ships (each with its own Wasp helicopter) were transformed into ambulance ships and performed a shuttle service.

Uganda left for the UK on 19 August. She had steamed over 22,000 miles, accepted 1,063 helicopter landings and admitted 730 battle casualties as in-patients, including 150 Argentinians, and the surgeons had carried out 554 operations.

Within hours of being requisitioned, SS Uganda (P&O) became the Task Force hospital ship. She accepted 730 battle casualties (including 150 Argentinians), and surgeons carried out 554 operations.

Sea King picking up a load from the deck of RFA *Black Rover*

Perhaps it is not always realised that helicopters are embarked in some of the larger Royal Fleet Auxiliary ships, and play a major part in the replenishment and protection of ships at sea when equipped for their ASW role. This was well illustrated in the Falklands campaign, and there was a further aspect. The fact that the Task Force had only two carriers meant that deck and hangar space was at a premium to accommodate the Harriers, and with the arrival of the additional aircraft from *Atlantic Conveyor*, some helicopters had to be moved out to make way for them. The RFAs had this hangar space and flight deck facility. By keeping these ships with the carrier battle group the Task Force commander was able to make use of them as an extension of his own carrier force.

Both 824 Squadron (with Sea Kings) and 845 and 847 (with Wessex HU5s) were deployed south in RFAs and, in the case of 847, a number were in *Atlantic Conveyor*. These aircraft were in constant demand to distribute and deliver stores between ships at sea and, where applicable, to take part in the ASW screen. On arrival at San Carlos they were deployed to the structural and physical limits of both aircraft maintainers and aircrew.

It is invidious to single out any one flight, but an 847 Squadron flight carried out over two thousand VERTREP missions in 450 hours of flying during the conflict. In 845 Squadron the records show that one flight made 1,084 deck landings in 427 hours of flying; and the 824 records state that one flight lifted over two thousand tons of stores in 650 hours of transfer operations. This was achieved in all kinds of weather at sea, and on land, in an inhospitable climate with winds, rain, sleet and snow to hamper the maintainers.

A Wessex HAS3 of 737 Naval Air Squadron operating her sonar as part of the screen for the carriers.

A helicopter from 824 Naval Air Squadron prepares to lift a load from RFA Black Rover *to deliver to a merchant ship in convoy.*

Sea King airlifting ammunition to 29 Commando Regiment

846 Naval Air Squadron flying Sea King HC 4 aircraft were ordered to support 3 Commando Brigade. During the eleven weeks of the campaign the squadron's total aircraft flying hours in their twelve aircraft totalled 3,107, during which they carried out 1,818 sorties. Four of the aircraft were equipped with PNG which enabled extensive operations to be carried out at night. Their 736 hours of night flying was a remarkable achievement – not only because of the strain of flying in pitch darkness close to the ground (for all concerned), but also because they were kept operational by the maintainers throughout the campaign.

On 10 June most of the squadron were operating from Teal Inlet in the north and this list of tasks for 10–13 June is typical of the whole of Operation Corporate:

10 June Lifting spares and stores to Rapier batteries at San Carlos, Teal and Fitzroy.
Inserting an SAS patrol in East Falkland and another in West Falkland.

11 June Squadron split between 3 Commando Brigade and 5 Infantry Brigade with six aircraft moving 2 Para from Fitzroy to Bluff Peak.
Nine PNG sorties for Special Forces carried out.

12 June Squadron flew guns and ammunition forward (now within range of enemy artillery).
One PNG sortie for Special Forces and night refuelling in a forward area.

13 June Further movement of guns and ammunition forward, interrupted by an attack by two Skyhawk aircraft. The pilot avoided destruction but a cannon shell passed through a rotor blade. A spare was flown up and fitted within two hours.

As the rate of advance continued the need for more aircraft became acute. The demand for shells to keep the guns in action seemed insatiable and towards the end it was one of the most serious problems facing the whole advance.

A 105mm gun of 29 Commando Regiment RA being moved to Mount Kent by a Sea King Mark 4 of 846 Naval Air Squadron.

A Sea King 5 of 820 Squadron delivering ammunition to the guns of 29 Commando Regiment RA below Mount Kent.

Chinook in whiteout conditions

'Bravo November' is a famous aircraft which, with its aircrews and maintenance detachment, played a distinguished part in the campaign. The aircraft was part of 18 Squadron Royal Air Force, only just re-formed with Chinook HC1 aircraft, previously having been equipped with Wessex HC2s. On 25 April five aircraft were flown to Portsmouth to be taken south in the *Atlantic Conveyor*. One aircraft was flown off at Ascension to assist with the massive air lift, while the remaining four sailed south with the ship. On 25 May the first aircraft ('Bravo November') was flown off to begin to resupply ships in company. *Atlantic Conveyor* was hit by one Exocet missile almost immediately afterwards, caught fire and had to be abandoned. With her went the three remaining Chinooks, no less than six Wessex 5s, a tented camp for 10,000 men and a huge supply of aircraft spares. For the rest of the campaign Bravo November operated from the San Carlos area of East Falkland.

Two aircrews and seventeen maintenance technicians remained with the aircraft but problems were not long in coming as all spare parts had been lost in *Atlantic Conveyor*. Despite this, and with no other aircraft to cannibalise, Bravo November remained operational throughout the conflict. Her work load was impressive. As an instance, on 30 May the aircraft carried three 105mm guns and twenty-two men forward to Mount Kent in one lift, the aircraft having to be kept in a low hover during disembarkation as the undercarriage had previously sunk into the peat on landing. On the return journey the weather worsened with snow flurries bringing visibility to zero. Travelling low and fast over ground possibly held by the enemy the aircraft momentarily hit the water of a creek, but the pilot was able to retain control and flew the helicopter clear. Possibly one of its more remarkable flights was when eighty-one fully armed men from 2 Para were crammed into the aircraft and taken forward to a position only ten miles from Port Stanley. The second load was only slightly less at seventy-five, exceeding the maker's specification in every way. Between 27 May and 14 June Bravo November flew 109 hours with no back-up spares, carried 2,150 troops and in excess of five hundred and fifty tons of stores and equipment.

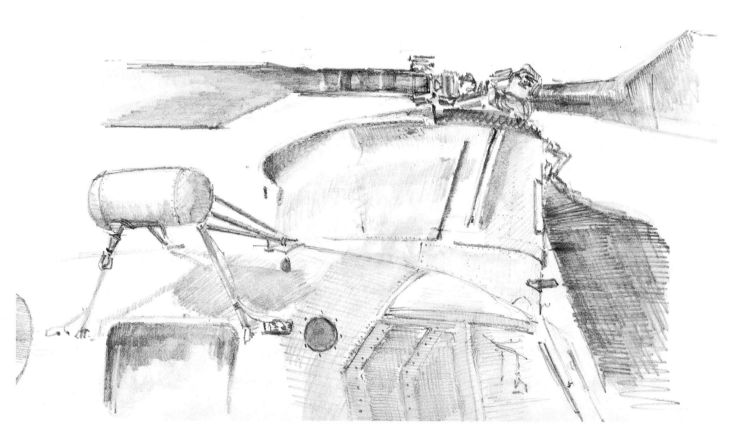

Detail of the rotors of a Mark 1 Chinook helicopter of 18 Squadron RAF.

'Bravo November' of 18 Squadron RAF was the only Chinook HC1 to operate with the Task Force during the campaign. This aircraft, with its extra lift capability, made an impressive contribution; she is seen here in a near whiteout as the pilot fights to retain control of the aircraft.

Falkland Sound

As soon as the decision was taken to sail a task force south, urgent consideration was given to the most effective area for a landing, should that become necessary. Three questions had to be asked: Where? When? and How?

Logistically suitable sites were available in a number of places, but at the outset, the positions of the Argentine defences were only a matter of speculation. The objective was to take Stanley, for this was obviously the headquarters and seat of government; but it was also certain to be defended. If the landings were made close to Stanley they would be opposed. The Task Force Commander had warned that it would not be possible to guarantee air superiority over the beach-head during the landings, which added weight to the need to avoid opposition at an early stage if at all possible. The problem was that the land forces wanted a short approach to Stanley, and thus short lines of communication, in an area where there were no roads and few tracks. Against this the naval requirement was an anchorage as secure as possible against the weather and Argentine air attacks, and of a sufficient area to accommodate the large number of ships which would support the actual landing. In the end it was the naval view which prevailed, and the alternatives

were whittled down to two. Either a landing should take place to the north, in the Port Salvador area which is a large inlet of water above Teal Inlet, or it should be in Falkland Sound itself. The final decision was in favour of Falkland Sound in the San Carlos area. There were a number of suitable beaches and two fine anchorages. Rising ground on all sides gave a defined perimeter which aided air defence and made missile attacks by enemy aircraft more difficult as their radar was at a disadvantage. However, it did mean that a long march lay ahead, and that the movement of stores over the virtually trackless terrain would pose very severe problems. Other drawbacks were an Argentine defensive position on Fanning Head, which controlled the entrance; an advance airfield on Pebble Island only sixteen miles away; and a known Argentine position in the Darwin/Goose Green area some twelve miles to the south west.

Turning to the question of timing, it seemed to the planners that there was no reason to delay, unless the Argentine Air Force was going to be destroyed, and that clearly was not happening. Added to that, winter was not far away and at all costs it was essential to reach Stanley before the bad weather set in. So it was decided not to wait until the arrival of 5 Infantry Brigade, but to land 3 Commando Brigade as soon as possible.

There now came the question of How? Admittedly there would not be opposition in any strength

to a landing, but equally there would not be British air superiority over the beach-head. The number of landing craft and helicopters was insufficient, and neither carrier could come inshore to become a helicopter platform. The decision was finally made for a night landing, using landing craft only. Before this could take place, the enemy position on Fanning Head had to be taken (see p. 44). Despite delays and some confusion, the landings and immediate consolidation took place without loss of life. There then followed an all-out race to land supplies, and helicopters worked round the clock. During the actual landing the San Carlos area was dominated by a protective screen of warships which allowed the troop transports to come close inshore and land the assault troops. Among them was the giant *Canberra*. As night fell on 21 May, *Canberra*, *Norland*, *Stromness* and *Europic Ferry* moved out of the Sound, having landed their troops and as much ammunition and equipment as could be handled in the day. The Argentines had launched between fifty and sixty sorties, and thirteen of their aircraft had been shot down, with three helicopters destroyed on the ground. British naval losses included *Ardent* sunk, together with *Brilliant*, *Antrim* and *Argonaut* damaged, and a total of twenty-seven servicemen killed. Miraculously, none of the large transports had been hit and the Commando Brigade was ashore.

During the next few days the battle for control of the skies over the anchorage continued. As more and more ships entered the Sound, their cargoes were distributed by landing craft and helicopter. The build-up of stores at Ajax Bay continued, and then as the troops advanced towards Stanley and the lines of communication increased, a forward base was established at Teal Inlet in preparation for the final assault.

Ships at anchor in Falkland Sound.

Ships at anchor in Falkland Sound, with a Lynx HAS2 from 815 Naval Air Squadron (Glasgow Flight).

Sea King in ASW role

AIR GUNNER.

Most of the Royal Navy's Sea Kings were fitted with general purpose machine guns at an early stage of the campaign. Normally they were mounted in the rear door.

In its logistical support and transport role, the Westland Sea King has a useful capacity. An added advantage is the fact that the canvas folding seats can be raised and stowed quickly without the need for the time-consuming business of seat removal. The resulting space is completely free from obstruction for the entire width of the aircraft, enabling 8000lb to be carried inside the fuselage.

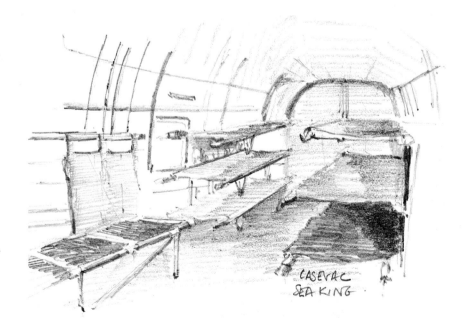

CASEVAC
SEA KING.

In addition to its anti submarine warfare role, the Westland Sea King's versatility enables fast internal modifications to be made. For casualty evacuation, two banks of three stretchers and twelve seats enable eighteen passengers to be accommodated, together with a rescue winch and spotlight.

The Sea King HAS5 is specially equipped to detect and destroy enemy submarines. Comparable to a frigate in its operational effectiveness in this role, it carries an impressive array of weapons. Deployed ahead of the Task Force, this aircraft of 820 Naval Air Squadron is operating its sonar equipment as it hovers forty feet above the sea.

Sea King with an underslung load over SS *Stena Seaspread*

Although many of the ships 'taken up from trade' (as requisitioning is called) were quickly fitted with helicopter platforms, space and the nature of this book do not allow adequate coverage of their service in the campaign. One example was SS *Stena Seaspread*, a North Sea oil rig maintenance and diving support vessel. Requisitioned on 10 April, she was modified in four and a half days and sailed on 16 April. After a few days in South Georgia (by now retaken) she moved to a position some two hundred miles east of the Falklands.

Stena Seaspread is an unusual vessel. She can remain stationary within three metres in up to a Force 9 gale, with a seventy-five per cent reduction in roll. Manned by twenty-nine men of the Merchant Navy, she embarked a diving team and other specialist engineers totalling 160 men, together with equipment for the major repair of battle-damaged ships. High above her bridge and accommodation superstructure was a large flight deck, but no hangar.

She was able to operate effectively in the open sea in difficult and uncomfortable weather conditions. HMS *Antrim* was her first customer, followed by *Glasgow*, which had a bomb pass through her engine room without exploding. HMS *Plymouth* had been damaged by four 1,000lb bombs, but was able to steam out to her for fuller repairs. The last ship to be assisted was the large destroyer HMS *Glamorgan*, hit by a land-fired Exocet missile which destroyed her hangar and Wessex helicopter, and her galley.

Other ships had helicopter platforms, some welded into place in a hurry, *QE2*, *Canberra* and *Elk*, *Norland* and *Geesport* being examples among many. Within hours of being requisitioned every ship with space to land a helicopter had preparations well in hand to build a platform. Co-operation between the dockyards, the Merchant Navy and the Royal Navy was such that problems were worked out with a remarkable absence of friction and the resulting achievement was impressive by any standards.

Helicopter deck
S.S. Stena Sea spread
1987

SS Stena Seaspread *was requisitioned from her job as a North Sea oil maintenance and diving support vessel. In her new role she embarked a clearance diving team and specialist engineers to repair major battle and storm damage. High above her bridge is a helicopter flight deck; here she is assisting HMS* Minerva *and RFA* Black Rover *while a Sea King HC4 from 846 Naval Air Squadron flies overhead.*

Scout helicopter in contact with a Scorpion tank

from 3 Troop
B Squadron
Blues & Royals (RHG/D)

The fact that nearly all the pilots of 3 Commando Brigade Air Squadron, and all those of 656 Squadron Army Air Corps, had military experience at troop and company level meant that they understood battle procedures and could support ground units effectively. The pilots were able to fly forward to exactly where they were needed. In the Goose Green battle every bomb and bullet not actually carried into battle or flown in by night by Sea King was carried forward by the squadron's helicopters. Every casualty, whether British or Argentine, was evacuated in the same way. The Gazelle had a homing facility, but the Scout did not. Despite this, night flying in an emergency was frequently undertaken. On more than one occasion the pilot was talked down in complete darkness, being given directions from the ground, his position being guessed from the sound of his engines.

As a result of the Goose Green battle, 3 CBAS allotted specific Gazelle helicopters to each unit in direct support, with the Scouts in reserve. Each had liaison officers with the unit so that precise instructions could be given. One of the features of this campaign, so different from forty years before, was the speed with which casualties were evacuated. The problem was that every time the aircraft flew forward it attracted artillery fire. It was a question of having the casualty ready for a quick landing and take off, but it is hard to overestimate the effect on morale of the knowledge that a man could be back at the Field Hospital within thirty to fifty minutes of being hit. During the closing twenty-four hours of the conflict, some eighty-five casualties were evacuated from the forward areas.

The handling and deployment of the aircraft was impressive. Being small and highly manoeuvrable they undertook a wide variety of work which in normal times was done by dispatch riders, jeeps or trucks. During the final day, three Scouts flew forward in support of 2 Para on Wireless Ridge on the outskirts of Stanley and fired SS 11 missiles at enemy gun positions. All three destroyed their targets.

A Scout HC1 helicopter lands to confer with the commander of a Scorpion tank of the Blues and Royals.

Wessex helicopter airlifting Royal Marines

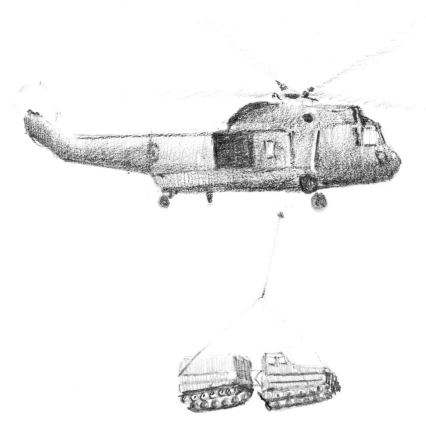

A Sea King helicopter lifting a bandwagon of the Commando Brigade Headquarters in an air lift during the closing stages of the campaign.

Although this is a 'helicopter story' it is not possible to tell that story adequately without some consideration of the troops and the loads that the helicopters carried. The Falkland Islands are two places. To those who leave a comfortable billet either in Stanley or at the garrison airfield at Mount Pleasant, the islands are bleak and barren and probably 'fit only for sheep' – without trees and with natural defences such as the stone rivers. These are collections of large boulders, which from a distance look like rivers of lava and are in fact two-ton lumps of rock, flung one on top of another in a crazy pattern and streaming down the hillsides. The

visitor looks to the hills and watches a solitary eagle soaring in the sky, or in the valleys he sees huge sea trout lying motionless in still waters. It may not be very hospitable, but it is perfectly tolerable.

To the men of the Parachute Regiment or of 45 Commando who had marched from San Carlos to Teal Inlet and now found themselves below Mount Kent it was a diabolically different story. To dig any form of slit trench was to breach the winter water table fourteen inches below the surface. To stand for any length of time in the same spot was to see brackish water oozing up over your boots. To withstand the unpredictable winds which allowed you to

build up some kind of shelter against rain or sleet or driving snow only to change 180 degrees in three minutes tried even the stoutest heart. Your feet were wet every day and your sleeping bag sodden and sometimes there was scarcely enough water to absorb your dehydrated rations because the water all round you was brackish and caused diarrhoea. Above all there was nowhere where you could climb in and get out of the cold and wet, with the added strain of carrying upwards of a hundred pounds on your back. That was the other Falklands, and those were the conditions that British troops of 3 Commando Brigade and latterly 5 Infantry Brigade accepted and survived. The horrific discomfort was overcome only by superb leadership, particularly at troop and section level and, in the end, by rugged individual courage.

However much those responsible for allocating the helicopters would wish to airlift clean dry socks or packs, the shortage of aircraft meant that rations and ammunition were simple priorities, and all else came only when supplies of these were complete. Ammunition and rations for the unit were usually landed centrally by helicopter. As night fell carrying parties converged to pick up and distribute the required rations and ammunition to isolated positions, sometimes over a considerable distance. This was a chore that everyone could have done without.

There is an item in a squadron's history which reads 'Airlifted 800 bergens'. By doing this the marines were spared the need to carry packs. They carried ammunition instead.

It is a measure of the quality of the British troops and the response by all those who supplied, maintained and flew the helicopters that the troops ashore survived the fiendish conditions which they had to overcome. It is in this context that the role of the maintainers can be viewed. Each aircraft which became unserviceable during the hours of daylight put the whole campaign in jeopardy. Over ninety per cent of the aircraft were operational throughout that period. Within just over three weeks these troops, and those who supplied them from the air, routed a force of superior numbers, dug in on defensive positions.

Airlifting mortars in preparation for the attack on Mount Harriet.

Maintaining helicopters in snow conditions

Weather conditions during the Falklands Campaign were of the sort most disliked both by the helicopters and by their crews. Moisture- and salt-laden air alternated with high winds and temperatures hovering around freezing. It was in those conditions that the maintainers fought to keep their aircraft operational. Prodigious feats of maintenance were carried out, including engine changes in the open. Possibly one of the more remarkable was when a Mark 4 of 846 Squadron had to land in a hurry after attack by an enemy fighter and the tail rotor assembly was damaged. Sometime earlier the undercarriage of an aircraft of 825 Squadron had penetrated the crust of the Falkland peat and the helicopter had toppled over. It was systematically cannibalised and the tail rotor was fitted to the 846 aircraft without the help of a crane, the job being performed with nothing more than muscle power and the aid of some packing cases. The aircraft returned to the squadron for the final advance to Stanley. The maintenance crews at work are shown in the four drawings below.

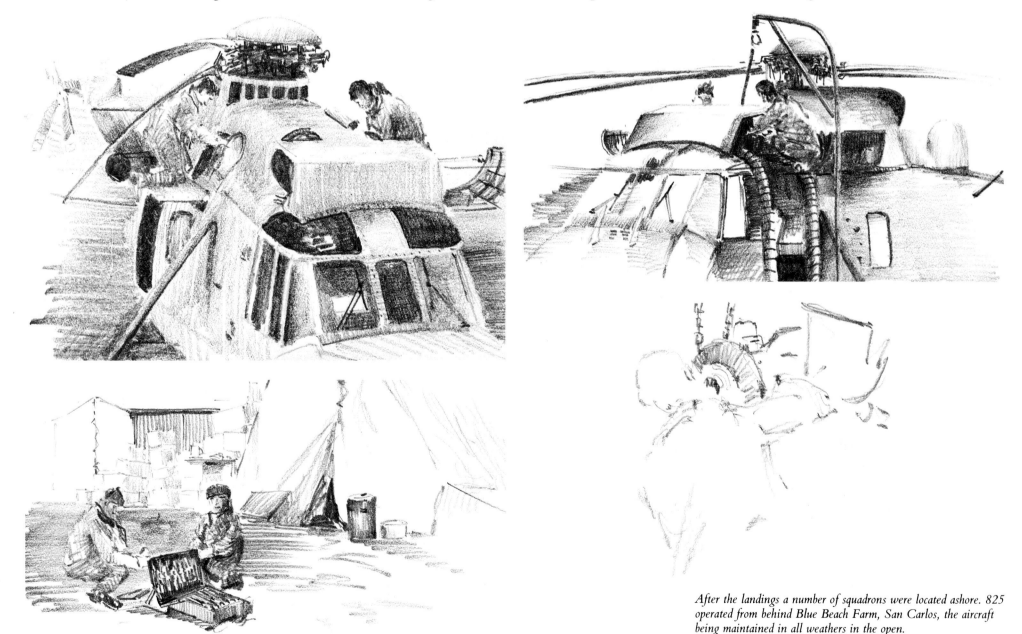

After the landings a number of squadrons were located ashore. 825 operated from behind Blue Beach Farm, San Carlos, the aircraft being maintained in all weathers in the open.

Sir Galahad rescue

Following the news that the Argentines had evacuated Fitzroy and Bluff Cove on the south coast, the 2nd Bn The Parachute Regiment was airlifted forward in one bold sweep to hold the south-west flank. The problem was that they were now isolated and it was essential that another brigade should move up fast. Unfortunately the area was visible from Stanley. Because of insufficient helicopter lift it was decided to sail the amphibious ships *Fearless* and *Intrepid* (on separate nights) to a position half way and transfer the troops to landing craft for the rest of the journey, thus allowing the ships to vacate the area before dawn. Half the 1st Bn The Welsh Guards arrived after a miserable seven hour spray-soaked passage in landing craft, but the next night conditions were worse. Those Welsh Guardsmen remaining in San Carlos were transferred to the landing ship *Sir Galahad*, which could reach Bluff Cove in the latter part of the night and be away again before dawn. However, the loading of 16 Field Ambulance took much longer than anticipated and the ship's departure was delayed, so her destination was changed to Fitzroy.

It is essential to give a fair and balanced account of the events leading up to the bombing of the *Sir Galahad* and that is not possible here. (Martin Middlebrook's *Task Force* (Penguin Books) gives a detailed and lucid account of what happened on the night of 7–8 June.) The present account opens with the arrival of the ship at Fitzroy and its sighting by the enemy. Within an hour Argentine aircraft had taken off to attack the ship together with the *Sir Tristram*, which was also there unloading ammunition. Five aircraft made the attack, damaging the *Sir Tristram*, but the attack on *Sir Galahad* was vastly more serious. One bomb exploded on the tank deck where most of the Welsh Guards were, together with tons of ammunition, and the area became filled with smoke and flame. Loss of all power resulted in darkness below decks as the men struggled to get out.

The fact that a television crew was on hand to film the rescue from *Sir Galahad* provided pictures that will never be forgotten. An aircraft of 825 Squadron which was in the area raised the alarm and the rescue began. Some life rafts had been launched, but they drifted against the ship's side and had to be blown clear by the down-draught of the helicopter rotors, but the main rescue area was in the fo'c'sle where most of the survivors had concentrated. The forward well and main cargo decks were ablaze, with thick smoke, and explosions took place every few seconds, brilliantly coloured smoke adding to the horror.

The helicopters hovered into this congested area one at a time, while others waited above. It was difficult and very hazardous to position the aircraft due to the continuous explosions which rocked them. It was a remarkable rescue accomplished in one hour with precision and professional expertise. Many of the survivors were badly burned or otherwise gravely injured and, having initially taken them to the nearby shore, there began the job of transferring them to the Field Hospital at Ajax Bay. That the casualty list which finally stood at fifty men killed and fifty-seven injured was not far greater was due in large measure to the helicopter crews.

The Sir Galahad *rescue. Aircraft are stacked up waiting to take off the Welsh Guards and ship's company as fires engulf the ship.*

The guns are moved forward

To those who have studied the land campaigns of 1939–45 and, of course, to those who took part, the three ton truck and the gunner's quod were the normal means of hauling guns and ammunition. In fact military transport was entirely dependent on the four-wheeled truck. In the '82 campaign there were no roads and no docks or cranes for unloading. The UK was nearly 8,000 miles away and the nature of the ground and the complete lack of buildings for shelter and storage added to the problems. Massed artillery support was quite out of the question because the rate of fire of the guns was beyond the logistic capacity of the supply of ammunition.

The Sea King 4 is a purpose-built helicopter capable of airlifting a 105mm gun and a small amount of ammunition, but to move a battery and sufficient ammunition to support a ground attack was out of the question without depriving the Land Force Commander of helicopter support in all other tasks. The aircraft were just not available in sufficient numbers. The difference between a Sea King and a Chinook is that the Sea King can lift one gun and the Chinook three. Thus, when allocating helicopters to 29 Commando Regiment RA, it was often a question of guns *or* ammunition and the problem had to be resolved by lifting a smaller number of guns with sufficient ammunition.

At the time of the Argentine surrender reinforcements were well on the way and a far more satisfactory build-up of air lift capacity was to become available, but at the moment when it was most needed it was insufficient for the task. It was indeed fortunate that the Argentine defence collapsed when it did.

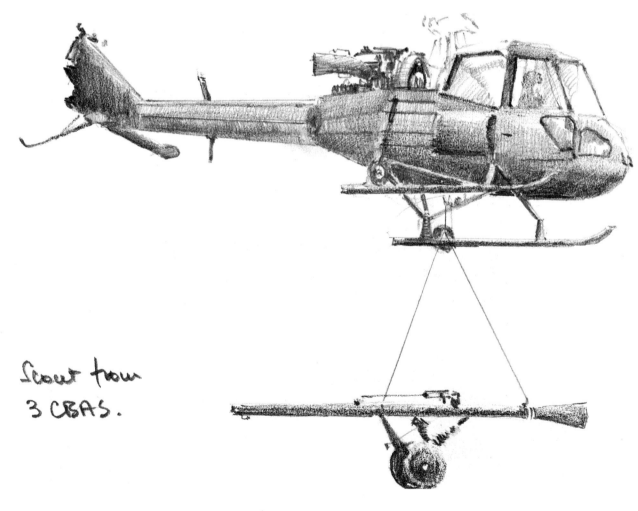

The guns are moved forward.

Casualty evacuation by Scout helicopter from Mount Tumbledown

The painting opposite is of but one incident during the conflict. A Scout helicopter from 656 Squadron Army Air Corps is flying fast over the crest of Tumbledown, having been in full view of the enemy and subjected to shell and machine-gun fire as it approached the Regimental Aid Post of the 2nd Bn The Scots Guards early on 13 June.

Although it is no consolation at all to the families of those who lost their lives, nonetheless the fact is that the fatal casualties sustained during the conflict were providentially light when compared with those of a generation ago, and one of the contributing factors for this was the policy of evacuation by helicopter. Another major consideration, and it should be recorded, was the length to which commanders went to minimise the loss of life. These two decisions were known throughout the land forces and contributed in no small measure to the remarkably high morale in atrocious conditions.

As has been seen, the Main Dressing Station was sited at Ajax Bay, and it was to there that casualties were evacuated before being made ready for their transfer to the hospital ship *Uganda* out at sea. As the advance approached Stanley the distance from Ajax Bay increased, and a Field Dressing Station was set up at Teal Inlet to act as a link. Forward in the battle area the Regimental Aid Posts could do little more than first aid, and it was there that Scout and Gazelle helicopters flew. On the outward journey they carried ammunition, and on their return casualties would be sat or laid in the back of the aircraft. If conscious, they were usually invited to hold their own or their chums' saline drips. While the pilot flew the helicopter the aircrewman did everything in his power to encourage and sustain the wounded during a short but often very bumpy and dangerous flight. The courage and professionalism of these aircrew were a by-word throughout the brigades. It is not difficult to understand the dangers they faced when taking off in darkness or first light and flying forward into an area made visible for miles around by the flashes of exploding shells, having been given a grid reference of the position of the wounded man or the Regimental Aid Post.

Casualty evacuation in the forward area. A Scout helicopter approaches to pick up a wounded paratrooper from Mount Longdon.

The helicopters of 3 CBAS and 656 Squadron Army Air Corps were in constant demand to evacuate wounded, sometimes from very exposed positions and under fire. Here a Scout AH1 of 656 Squadron AAC is about to land on Mount Tumbledown in the early morning to evacuate wounded Scots Guardsmen.

Southern Thule. Helicopters operating in bad weather

An analysis of the aircraft losses during the campaign is an important part of the story of the helicopters. In all thirty-five aircraft were lost by British forces from all causes, twenty-five of them helicopters. Of these twenty-five, ten went down with the *Atlantic Conveyor* and two with the sinking of the *Coventry* and *Ardent*. *Broadsword*'s Lynx was severely damaged when she was hit by a bomb, and *Glamorgan*'s Lynx was destroyed in the Exocet attack. One aircraft was destroyed by its crew on landing on Chilean territory. This now accounts for fourteen destroyed, leaving eleven.

On the Fortuna Glacier in South Georgia two aircraft were lost in blizzards, though no one was hurt, but the loss of a Sea King with twenty-one servicemen was grievous. In addition three aircraft were lost operationally in accidents: two, when in the hover, lost power, and one crashed on a return flight to *Hermes* after a VERTREP. In this case the aircrewman was drowned.

This leaves four helicopters, all from 3 CBAS and all lost due to direct action in the air. One Scout was lost on a CASEVAC mission to 2 Para at Darwin when it was shot down by a Pucara aircraft and the pilot was killed. The three remaining were all Gazelles; two were shot down within minutes of each other by small arms fire over enemy territory and the aircrews were all killed. The last was due to a tragic error during a flight in East Falkland when the aircraft was accidentally targeted by a British Seadart missile and all four occupants were killed.

Considering the intensity of the operational duties of the helicopters, the losses were mercifully few.

Southern Thule lies 450 miles to the southeast of South Georgia, within the Antarctic Circle. The last Argentine presence on British territory was a weather station which had been based on the island since 1976. On 17 June, after the ceasefire, the frigate *Yarmouth*, with the RFA *Olmeda*, proceeded to South Georgia, embarked two troops of 42 Commando and was met by HMS *Endurance*, with a Wessex 5 embarked, and the tug *Salvageman*. This small force, with six helicopters, landed a detachment of Royal Marines in the vicinity of the weather station. At the same time other helicopters were made to simulate further landings. At dawn next day these men were ordered to advance down towards the weather station. The detachment of Argentines surrendered six minutes before the *Yarmouth* was due to open fire in a spectacular bombardment of an outcrop of rock not far from the weather station. The station was then blown up.

Aircrewman.

Southern Thule. After it was all over, the last Argentine troops, manning a weather station on Southern Thule in the South Sandwich Islands, were taken off and returned to Argentina. The operation took place in winter amid snow and high winds.

Treasures of
Bob Dylan

Brian Southall

CARLTON

Contents

Introduction by Brian Southall

It seems appropriate that as part of an introduction, I should mention how Bob Dylan first came into my life. As with for so many other British teenagers in the heady days of the 1960s, it was through his second album *The Freewheelin' Bob Dylan* and its peace anthems and protest songs. I bought it, played it incessantly and also studied the front cover photo of Bob and his girlfriend walking arm-in-arm down a snow-covered street in New York. That was in 1963, and in February 1977 when I first visited New York (I was head of press at EMI and there with Queen) the journalist Mick Brown took me to the very same street to pay homage to the spirit of Bob Dylan ... and magically it was still covered in six inches of snow.

Earlier, when I was a journalist on a local newspaper, I went along to see Dylan at London's Royal Albert Hall. It was 1965 – the year before he went 'electric' – and for reasons known only to my editor, I was allowed to review the concert ... and claim the rail fare on expenses.

I told my readers that "he showed great talent and that not everybody needs a full orchestral backing or an electric guitar" and that he entertained a packed house with "just plain talent and originality." In my maddest moments I like to think that maybe I played a small part in ensuring that his career would run on for another five decades!

My affection has continued to the present day although I now accept that he is entitled to use an electric guitar if he wants to and I also know that his live shows are as likely to be a disappointment as they are a joy. Earls Court in 1978 was one of the joyous moments while London Docklands Arena in 2002 was ... let's just say we left early!

The Beatles' love and respect for Dylan has been well documented and while one writer suggested that "Without Bob Dylan rock 'n' roll as we know it would not exist," another described him as "The most influential folk/rock vocalist/composer ever." On the other hand, those who have worked on releasing and promoting his albums have occasionally taken a different view.

One CBS executive who spent time backstage waving the corporate flag during Dylan's visits to the UK recounts, "He really couldn't give a toss about whether we turned up or not. He's not remotely interested." While the same man acknowledges the genius of Bob Dylan, he also retains a vivid recollection of his meetings with the great man. "He was never charming and was basically a curmudgeonly old fuck."

Walter Yetnikoff, the man who ran CBS in America, was another executive who saw the unhelpful and unresponsive side of Dylan but he never let it bother him. "If he wanted to sulk in the corner, let him sulk in the corner," was his philosophy.

At the same time, multi-million selling singer Mick Hucknall acknowledges the value of Dylan's simplistic attitude to the music business. "He has enhanced his image as the wandering troubadour by just touring, playing and recording and not really bothering about the media."

The story goes that when former Bananarama and Shakespear's Sister singer Siobhan Fahey was married to Dave Stewart, Dylan joined them for dinner one night. During the evening Dylan contributed almost nothing to the conversation and when Mrs Stewart asked her husband, "What do you think is going on in there?" the former Eurythmics star said simply, "Everything."

Bob Dylan is undoubtedly an enigmatic genius and he has perhaps deliberately created an aura of indifference and even rudeness in order to keep away those aspects of fame and success which he considers unnecessary, skittish and wearisome.

British guitarist Mick Ronson joined Dylan's Rolling Thunder tour in 1975 and told people he was convinced that Dylan never knew his name and insisted on referring to him – both on and off stage – as simply "the Limey."

On the other hand Bob Dylan does have an interest in everyday things such as shopping and recreation. My only close encounter with him took place on the street in London's Mayfair in 1978, when he was on his way to an up-market clothes shop.

He was with CBS press officer Elly Smith and I made my way over in order to meet her escort. I said hello – there was no handshake – and for the next five or six minutes I rambled on about the impact Dylan and his music had had on me and how I was looking forward to seeing him on stage. While I spoke, and Elly chipped in with some observations, Dylan said nothing ... absolutely nothing, not even goodbye!

Ms Smith was also the person who had to arrange a spot of physical recreation for Dylan during that 1978 visit. His hotel didn't have a pool so she called up a larger five-star hotel to ask if Mr. Dylan could come down for a dip. "He didn't want the pool cleared or anything but I did ask for a time when it might be quiet," she recalls. "We got there and went into the pool which was completely empty except for all the cleaning staff who were standing on the side with their mops and brooms just watching Bob Dylan swim."

For another former record company executive it was time spent with Alice Cooper in 1991 which yielded an unexpected Dylan moment. "I arranged to play golf with Alice at Wentworth and he said he was going to bring a friend," explains Paul Russell. "I told him I needed to know his name a day or so before and when Alice called, he said he was bringing Bob Dylan." Russell got another CBS artist to make up a foursome – "a Welsh guy who was so gobsmacked to be playing with Alice Cooper and Bob Dylan that he couldn't hit a ball all day" – and gave his two most famous guests their dress code. "I told them they had to wear golf hats and no trainers were allowed in the club house and they turned up with all the right clothing and equipment but we sat outside. They both kept their caps on and nobody recognized them. Bob took it very seriously and played very well, although Alice won."

Singer, songwriter, performer, protester, swimmer and golfer – you can choose your own Bob Dylan image. For me he remains one of the few genuinely inspirational artists ever to enter the world of popular music ... even if he did ignore me. But then I'd forgive him everything for just a handful of his songs which have thankfully found their way into my life.

The Early Years

Though now more than 70, Bob Dylan has never lost his simple yearning to make music, though fame, fortune and commerciality sometimes threatened to dam the pure stream of his creativity: a stream that rose in his formative years, in what was, prior to the addition of Alaska, America's most northerly state.

Robert Allen Zimmerman was born on May 24, 1941, in the Midwestern town of Duluth, Minnesota, and from the age of six was raised in the nearby town of Hibbing, a once prosperous iron mining community close to Lake Superior. Water plays a big part in Minnesota's history; the state, which borders mainland Canada, takes its name from a Native American word meaning "Land of a thousand lakes."

Although he was born seven months before America entered World War Two, following the Japanese bombing of Pearl Harbor, Dylan once reflected on what it meant to come into the world in the midst of warfare and with the threat of invasion hanging in the air: "If you were born around that time or were living and alive, you could feel the old world go and the new one beginning."

At school, many of his teachers were the same people who had taught his mother and, as Dylan approached his teenage years, the Cold War and the Iron Curtain focused American fears on the threat of a Russian invasion, which according to Dylan was a genuine fear in his home state. "The Reds were everywhere – we were told – and out for blood lust," he said.

Growing up, Dylan discovered the radio and quickly became fascinated by blues and country music before becoming engrossed, in the mid-1950s, by the fast-emerging phenomenon that was rock'n'roll. From listening to records on the radio the young Dylan turned to playing music live and his earliest attempts were with bands called The Jokers (formed in a Jewish summer camp), The Show Boaters and The Golden Chords.

Schoolwork regularly took a back seat as the young Zimmerman took off to go on the road as a carny ("I was with the carnival on and off for six years"), where he worked on rides such as the Ferris wheel. "I didn't go to school for a bunch of years," he admitted, before adding: "It all came out even, though." He eventually graduated from Hibbing High School aged 18, just a few months after he'd seen Buddy Holly perform in Duluth. Five days after the show at the town's National Guard Armory, Holly died in a plane crash in neighbouring Iowa, aged just 22.

The young Dylan was a fan of the bespectacled Texan, but soon

ABOVE Dylan's home in Seventh Avenue, Hibbing, Minnesota, which has been renamed Bob Dylan Drive.

ABOVE A postcard from Hibbing giving pride of place to the town's (and Bob Dylan's) High School.

moved on to discover the Everly Brothers before returning to the one performer who, for him, stood head and shoulders above all others. The piano-playing youngster who called himself Bobby Zimmerman had discovered Richard Penniman and the joys of 'Tutti Frutti' and 'Lucille'." So impressed was Zimmerman that his 1959 high school yearbook entry lists his ambition as "to follow Little Richard."

Another major turning-point came in the same year when Zimmerman, who had taken to calling himself Elston Gunn, made his way to Fargo in nearby North Dakota and made contact with local act Bobby Vee and the Shadows. He talked himself into a job as a backing pianist on a few local shows, for a total of $30, but when he got back home he bragged that he'd actually played piano on Vee's US Top 100 hit 'Suzie Baby', even though it was recorded before he joined the band. Those locals familiar with young Master Gunn soon came to realize that he would often change names and confuse fact and fiction when he recounted his experiences.

It was time to stretch his wings, and Zimmerman left for the city of Minneapolis, and Minnesota State University. It was here that he began to move away from rock'n'roll and focus his attention on his country's folk music. "I knew that when I got into folk music, it was a more serious type of thing," he explained later. "The songs are

filled with more despair, more sadness, more triumphs, more faith in the supernatural, much deeper feelings."

Fuelled by his new-found love of folk, and the music of artists such as Woody Guthrie, Pete Seeger, Odetta and Dave Van Ronk, Gunn/Zimmerman began to appear on Minneapolis' folk circuit, in the Dinkytown district close to the university. And here a new name began to emerge.

"You call yourself what you want to call yourself," he explained. "This is the land of the free." So Robert Zimmerman, now Elston Gunn, toyed with becoming Robert Allen or Robert Alleyn, while rejecting both Robert Dylan and Bobby Dylan – stories say the new surname was inspired by either the Welsh poet Dylan Thomas, a distant relation named Dillon or even the American TV lawman Marshal Matt Dillon – in favour of Bob Dylan. At one point Dylan contemplated Woody as a first name in honour of his new-found hero Woody Guthrie, whose songs, such as 'This Land Is Your Land', 'Tom Joad' and 'Grand Coulee Dam', he enthusiastically added to his list of titles as he learnt to master the guitar and harmonica. It was his determination to meet the Oklahoma-born sometime hobo and regular busking musician Guthrie that convinced Dylan to leave Minnesota and make his way east to New Jersey and New York City.

RIGHT Dylan was inspired to play the harmonica by folk singer and protester Woody Guthrie.

New York City

Bob Dylan was so in thrall to the music - the cause of America's poor and the legend that was Woodrow Wilson Guthrie - that in late 1960 he travelled close to 1,500 miles to meet him.

Perhaps in tribute to the man who himself crisscrossed America riding free in railway boxcars, Dylan even told people he journeyed from Minnesota to New York on a freight train, although he later admitted: "What I did was come across country from the Midwest in a four-door sedan, '57 Impala." Making his way to New York was all about music: "I was here to find singers, the ones I'd heard on record – but most of all to find Woody Guthrie."

Dylan arrived in New York in late January 1961 and within a few days was at the Greystone Park Hospital in New Jersey where Guthrie, 48, was being treated for Huntington's chorea, a hereditary disease that had killed his mother. There Dylan chatted with and even sang to his hero before leaving with the inspiration to write a song. 'Song To Woody' was, according to Dylan, "the first song I ever wrote that I performed in public."

New York's Greenwich Village offered the young man from Minnesota every opportunity to develop his art and pursue his dream. In clubs, bars and coffee houses such as Café Wha?, The Gaslight, Gerde's Folk City and The Kettle of Fish, Dylan saw and met the people he had come to find – Dave Van Ronk, Richie Havens, Josh White, Brownie McGhee and Sonny Terry and the Seegers – Pete, Peggy and Mike.

Playing afternoon gigs for a dollar and a cheeseburger, Dylan

ABOVE On the bill as support for John Lee Hooker in April 1961.

FAR LEFT Dylan accompanies Karen Dalton and Fred Neil in the Café Wha? in 1961.

LEFT The hugely influential Woody Guthrie with his famous 'Fascists' guitar entertains his fellow travellers on the New York subway.

began to forge a path in New York's Bohemian hotspot. He supported John Lee Hooker and played harmonica on sessions for Harry Belafonte before a Folk City show in September 1961, where he was seen and praised by influential *New York Times* music critic Robert Shelton. The review caught the eye of legendary CBS/Columbia producer and talent scout John Hammond who, after hiring Dylan to accompany singer Carolyn Hester, offered him a recording contract. Hammond's involvement with the likes of Billie Holiday, Count Basie, Bessie Smith and Benny Goodman was well known to Dylan, who put pen to paper without a second glance: "I would have gladly signed whatever form he put in front of me."

As he prepared to go into the studio, Dylan played a showcase at New York's celebrated Carnegie Chapter Hall to an audience of just 53. Undeterred, he and Hammond recorded *Bob Dylan* in just two days, November 20 and 22, 1961. As yet without a portfolio of his own songs, Dylan was obliged to search for material for his eponymous debut release. Time spent in the folk clubs of New York had opened his ears to a wide selection of authentic traditional music, and he opted to arrange four of the final 13 songs himself.

'In My Time Of Dyin", 'Man Of Constant Sorrow', 'Pretty Peggy-O' and 'Gospel Plow' joined Dave Van Ronk's arrangement of 'House Of The Rising Sun', Roy Acuff's treatment of 'Freight Train Blues' and Eric Von Schmidt's arrangement of 'Baby Let Me Follow You Down' alongside Jesse Fuller's 'You're No Good', Bukka White's 'Fixin' To Die', Curtis Jones' 'Highway 51' and 'See That My Grave Is Kept Clean' by Blind Lemon Jefferson, to create the bulk of the album.

To complete his debut Dylan added two of his own songs, 'Talkin' New York Blues' and his tribute 'Song To Woody'. Four other songs – 'House Carpenter', 'He Was A Friend Of Mine' and Guthrie's 'Ramblin' Man Blues', plus Dylan's third original song from the period, 'Man On The Street' – missed the final track selection.

According to Hammond, his new find was somewhat less than the perfect recording artist; besides problems with his enunciation of the letters P and S, Dylan regularly wandered "off mic,"

In March 1962, *Bob Dylan* hit the shops, while the accompanying first single, 'Mixed Up Confusion', hit the airwaves. Neither album nor single, which was swiftly withdrawn by Columbia, made the US charts (the album did peak at number 13 in the UK three years on), but they did create a stir around the city's folk circuit where Dylan's shows were becoming a major draw.

Before the year was out Dylan decided to change his name legally to Bob Dylan, while at the same time signing a management deal with Albert Grossman. Of those two decisions one would last the rest of the decade, the other a lifetime.

ABOVE Some very rare, bootleg examples of Dylan's earliest known (1960s) recordings.

RIGHT Dylan pauses for thought during his debut recording sessions for Columbia.

Bob Dylan
Released March 1962. Tracks: You're No Good, Talkin' New York Blues, In My Time Of Dyin', Man Of Constant Sorrow, Fixin' To Die, Pretty Peggy-O, Highway 51, Gospel Plow, Baby Let Me Follow You Down, House Of the Rising Sun, Freight Train Blues, Song To Woody, See That My Grave Is Kept Clean.

The Freewheelin' Bob Dylan
and The Times They Are A-Changin'

In December 1962 Dylan travelled to Britain for the first time at the invitation of TV director Philip Saville, who had seen him perform in Greenwich Village. He had Dylan in mind for the role of Bobby the Hobo in a TV play called *Madhouse On Castle Street.*

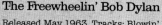

The Freewheelin' Bob Dylan

Released May 1963. Tracks: Blowin' In The Wind, Girl From The North Country, Masters Of War, Down the Highway, Bob Dylan's Blues, A Hard Rain's A-Gonna Fall, Don't Think Twice It's Alright, Bob Dylan's Dream, Oxford Town, Talking World War III Blues, Corinna Corinna, Honey Just Allow Me One More Chance, I Shall Be Free

While in London Dylan sang in folk clubs and pubs such as the Troubadour, Bunjies, Les Cousins and the King And Queen and in January, during his last week in England, he went into the studio to supply backing vocals on an album by Dick Farina and Eric Von Schmidt – credited as Blind Boy Grunt. His trip also brought him into contact with traditional British songs such as 'Scarborough Fair' and 'Lady Franklin's Lament', which would stay with him when he began work on his second album.

As recording got under way, manager Grossman attempted to have Hammond replaced as Dylan's producer but, despite major differences of opinion and attitude, Hammond stayed, although jazz producer Tom Wilson joined the project.

Recording began in April and the album was completed a year later, in April 1963, with 11 songs credited as Dylan compositions; he was emerging as the creator of his own music, with an eye towards social change.

There are many stand-out tracks on the album that would appear in May 1963 as *The Freewheelin' Bob Dylan*, with Don Hunstein's evocative cover shot of Dylan and girlfriend Suze Rotolo walking near their apartment on West 4th Street.

'Blowin' In The Wind' was written in The Commons, a Greenwich coffee house, in April 1962. Seen as a universal protest song for a new generation, he explained it thus: "I'm only 21 years old and I know that there's been too many wars … you people over 21 should know better." It was the first Dylan song to make it into the charts, when folk trio Peter, Paul and Mary (also managed by Grossman) took it into the top 10 in both the US and the UK.

'Girl From The North Country,' first conceived back in the late 1950s, was eventually completed with 'Scarborough Fair' as its basis. He wrote the lyrics down in late 1962 and finished it in Italy the following January.

'A Hard Rain's A-Gonna Fall' began as a long free verse poem and,

thanks in part to the Cuban missile crisis of 1962, became a youth anthem. While denying the "hard rain" was nuclear fallout, Dylan said: "I don't really care to define what I do."

'Don't Think Twice It's Alright' was one of his earliest love songs, inspired by Rotolo, but was taken into the American Top 10 by Peter, Paul and Mary in 1963 and into the British Top 10 by Dylan himself in 1965. Dylan's next girlfriend, singer Joan Baez, performed it in 1963 and, referring to Rotolo, announced it as a song "about a love affair that has lasted too long."

The album brought Dylan his first real taste of commercial success when it went gold in America and reached number 22 in the US charts. In the UK it would top the charts for two weeks in April 1965.

August 1963 saw Dylan back in Columbia's Studio A in New York, and this time Wilson was the sole producer in charge of recording the 11 new songs delivered by Dylan, by now a popular and influential figure – even if Wilson started with some reservations. "I didn't particularly like folk music. I thought folk music was for dumb old guys. This guy played like the dumb guys. But then these words came out!"

Prophetically entitled *The Times They Are A-Changin'*, it was recorded between August and October and focused on the major issues affecting America and the world – racism, poverty and injustice. The title track – once described as "a battle hymn for a generation" – was completed in the last week of recording and was Dylan's first UK single release in the spring of 1965. Melody Maker reviewer Ray Coleman told his readers that Dylan was "more a commentator than a singer," before adding, "You can't dance to it. But you CAN think to it." The single – described by Dylan as: "A song with a purpose. I wanted to write a big song: some kind of theme song" – hit the UK Top 10.

'With God On Our Side' was completed on the second day – August 7, 1963 – and joined the track listing as one of the decade's starkest protest anthems.

ABOVE Cigarette in hand, Dylan poses for the camera.

RIGHT Bob Dylan and Joan Baez – they were partners both on and off stage.

'One Too Many Mornings' was the most personal song in a collection made up mainly of protest tracks; and it described the end of his relationship with Rotolo. It was recorded during the same session as the title track. His by then former girlfriend also inspired the song 'Boots Of Spanish Leather'.

'The Lonesome Death Of Hattie Carroll', one of Dylan's earliest reportage songs, focuses on an event in Baltimore on February 9, 1963, when black waitress Carroll, a mother of 11, died of a brain haemorrhage attributed to stress following a drunken assault by wealthy, spoilt local 24-year-old William Zantzinger. He stood trial for murder but was found guilty of manslaughter and sentenced to six months in prison.

Released in January 1964, in the aftermath of John F Kennedy's assassination and Martin Luther King's "I have a dream" speech, the album reached number 20 in America, but would eventually, in April 1965, hit number 4 in the UK.

Political Dylan

Dylan and politics were never far apart as he consistently strove to make his voice heard, and in May 1963 – just as his debut album was being released across America – he made his first very public stand against authority, taking as his inspiration earlier musicians with a conscience and a message, including Woody Guthrie, Pete Seeger and Odetta.

Invited on to the hugely influential primetime *Ed Sullivan Show* – produced by the television arm of his record company, CBS – Dylan was all set to sing 'Talkin' John Birch Paranoid Blues' when a station executive suggested he perform another song for fear of libelling the John Birch Society, a radical right-wing political group strongly opposed to communism and civil rights and named after a Baptist missionary and US intelligence officer shot by communists in China in 1945. Dylan would not agree to the censorship and refused to appear on the show, which led to reports in the New York Times, Billboard and Village Voice. The song itself had been recorded for inclusion on Dylan's debut album *The Freewheelin' Bob Dylan* but was cut at some stage, although there is no hard evidence this was done as a direct result of the TV show incident.

Fresh from his dispute with CBS TV, Dylan flew south to Mississippi to join Pete Seeger at a black voter registration rally in the aftermath of the murder of black civil rights organizer Medgar Evers.

There in Greenwood he sang the song 'Only A Pawn In Their Game' for the first time.

Alongside fellow-singer and protester Joan Baez, Dylan continued to champion the burgeoning civil rights movement and they both song 'With God On Our Side' at the 1963 Newport Folk Festival before joining the momentous March to Washington in August 1963 when 200,000 people – led by Martin Luther King – gathered to protest for jobs, justice and peace. Dylan performed 'Blowin' In the Wind' and left America's capital city as "the voice of a generation."

These events were very much the inspiration for Dylan's outpouring on his album *The Times They Are A-Changin'*, although he did declare in 1963: "I don't think what comes out of my music is a call to action," and added a couple of years later: "Songs aren't going to save the world." Whether he was right or not, it was a fact that the music of Bob Dylan was now playing a major role in shaping the thoughts and actions of people all around the globe.

With the assassination of President Kennedy in November 1963, the chances of someone taking a pot-shot at Dylan began to increase. In response, he made a point of reiterating that he wasn't a protest singer and made himself less available and less visible, hoping he wouldn't be singled out as the supposed spokesman for white,

ABOVE In front of the camera before refusing to appear on *The Ed Sullivan Show*.
LEFT Dylan playing in Mississippi in 1963 at a black voter rally.

RIGHT Bob Dylan, Joan Baez and Paul Stookey perform in front at the Lincoln Memorial in 1963.

middle-class activists and protesters.

Though still shaken by Kennedy's murder, the following month Dylan agreed to accept the Tom Paine Award at the annual Bill of Rights dinner in Washington. Given in honour of English-born author, pamphleteer, radical and intellectual Thomas Paine, who emigrated to America in 1774 to become one of the Founding Fathers of the United States, the award had gone to philosopher Bertrand Russell in 1962.

Uncomfortable, and perhaps even regretting having attended,

Dylan got drunk and turned on the organizers, the Emergency Civil Liberties Committee, questioning their role and their members. He was booed and hissed, and later apologized for his actions via a prose poem, but he wasn't finished, and later suggested that the audience that night "had nothing to do with my kind of politics."

Dylan's political passion lay in bringing injustice, warmongering, poverty and racism to the forefront of mainstream America's consciousness. He'd done it through songs about the killing of Hattie Carroll and Medgar Evers and also in 'The Death of Emmett Till',

a black man murdered in Mississippi in 1955, while in 'With God On Our Side', 'Masters Of War' and 'A Hard Rain's A-Gonna Fall' he made clear his feelings about weapons and the military and, with 'The Times They Are A-Changin'' and 'Talkin' John Birch Paranoid Blues', he took his stand in favour of civil rights.

But by the end of 1963 Dylan stood at a crossroads, and there were those who believed things were about to change, as they spotted signs that Dylan was losing patience with the increasing organization of the protest movement.

Another Side Of Bob Dylan

The next album, his fourth in as many years, was to be the first in a series that showed Dylan in a new, softer and more personal light. Aptly entitled *Another Side Of Bob Dylan*, it drew criticism from the folk community who sensed they might be losing their main man. Accused of being caught up with fame and out of touch with the times, Dylan did appear to be relinquishing his mantle as spokesman for America's angry youth, confirming to New Yorker magazine that "there ain't any finger-pointin' songs" on his new album.

He wrote some of the songs during a three-week road trip across America with friends Paul Clayton, Victor Maymudes and Pete Jarman in February 1964. They drove south from New York to visit first New Orleans, then Dallas, where they saw the spot where Kennedy had been shot, before turning west to head for Los Angeles and San Francisco.

According to Dylan the trip was about "talking to people – that's where it's at, man," but he also found time, seated in the back seat of the station-wagon with his typewriter, to create both songs and poetry.

In May, before recording began, Dylan briefly crossed the Atlantic for his first major British concert, at the Royal Festival Hall. The trip also served to promote the three albums already in his catalogue, and Dylan was interviewed by a select few British journalists. One, from New Musical Express, got an insight into Dylan's style of songwriting: "The words come first. Then I fit a tune or just strum the chords. Really, I'm no tune-writer. The songs for me are very confining, or something." Asked about the idea of British singers performing blues, soul or American folk, Dylan said: "If an English singer's happy singing a Southern US ballad, I'd rather see him being happy than see him doing something else and being unhappy."

For the show, on Sunday, May 17, Dylan opted to sing 18 of his own songs, although there remains some mystery over the final set

ABOVE A pensive Dylan takes a break (**ABOVE RIGHT**), before adopting a far away look for a more posed shot.

list. The Performing Right Society form shows three tracks listed only as "new song", and it's possible these were previously unheard tracks from his forthcoming album.

From London, Dylan travelled to Paris, where he met a German model named Christa Paffgen, who was later to find fame with The Velvet Underground as Nico. While they were together in Greece, Dylan put the finishing touches to many of the songs destined for the album.

Back in New York, Columbia quickly allocated him studio time with producer Tom Wilson and, astonishingly, he finished the album in a single day. In fact, in just one session, in Studio A on June 9, 1964, during which Dylan drank two bottles of Beaujolais, recorded 14 original songs and selected 11 for *Another Side Of Bob Dylan*. Being organized, it seems, was a key part of his recording process, as Wilson observed: "He always had his songs written out when he came into the studio."

'All I Really Want To Do', completed after returning from Europe, was one of Dylan's most lighthearted songs and was taken into the UK Top five by The Byrds, while in America Cher's version made the top 20.

The symbolic 'Black Crow Blues' was also completed in New York; with Dylan adding piano to his familiar guitar and harmonica. It was completed alongside 'Spanish Harlem Incident', a story of new romance featuring some of the writer's most unusual word couplings.

'Chimes Of Freedom' was written during Dylan's road trip after meeting civil rights activists Cordell Reagon and Bernice Johnson in Atlanta. His lyrics reflect the writer's new-found muse, French poet Arthur Rimbaud.

'My Back Pages' was the last track recorded during the mammoth one-day session, which ended at 1.30am, and contains some of Dylan's finest lyrics including the reflective line about his life so far: "I was so much older then, I'm younger than that now."

'To Ramona' was written in Greece, though about whom remains a topic for debate; one interpretation is that the subject is Joan Baez, and that the song makes reference to her desire to remain part of the folk movement Dylan had rejected.

'Ballad In Plain D' describes his parting from Suze Rotolo in 1964, partly as a result of his relationship with Baez. One of Dylan's most vicious, self-pitying songs, some critics have suggested it should have been left off the album, or never recorded at all.

'It Ain't Me Babe' again focuses on the break-up of his relationship with Rotolo and may have been written while they were apart during Dylan's brief UK tour in March 1964. The Turtles took the song into the US top 10 in 1965, while Johnny Cash hit the US top 30 with it in the same year.

It may have been Dylan himself who decided it would be the final track on what would be his last acoustic album, although producer Wilson saw a new opportunity: "I said if you put some background to this you might have a white Ray Charles with a message." Perhaps reflecting the less protest-orientated nature of the album, *Another Side Of Bob Dylan* edged into the US top 50 during 1964 while in the UK, on the back of his debut show, it reached number eight.

Another Side Of Bob Dylan
Released August 1964. Tracks: All I Really Want To Do, Black Crow Blues, Spanish Harlem Incident, Chimes Of Freedom, I Shall Be Free #10, To Ramona, Motorpsycho Nightmare, My Back Pages, I Don't Believe You, Ballad In Plain D, It Ain't Me Babe.

BOB DYLAN AT PHILHARMONIC HALL

ONLY NEW YORK CONCERT APPEARANCE ON SATURDAY OCTOBER 31ST AT 8:30PM

ALL SEATS RESERVED: $4.50, 4.00, 3.50, 2.75
ON SALE NOW AT PHILHARMONIC BOX OFFICE
Mail Orders To Philharmonic Hall, B'way at 65 St N.Y. 10023
INCLOSE STAMPED SELF-ADDRESSED ENVELOPE

COLUMBIA RECORDS

LEFT A poster advertising Dylan as top of the bill in New York's Philharmonic Hall on Hallowe'en Night in 1964.

ABOVE With four albums under his belt, Dylan was playing to sellout concerts on both sides of the Atlantic Ocean.

Bringing It All Back Home

By the time *Another Side Of Bob Dylan* was finished, Dylan knew he had to move on from his accepted role as a protest singer.

Most of summer 1964 was spent in Woodstock in upstate New York, where Grossman had a house. August's visitors included Joan Baez, who noted: "Most of the month or so we were there Dylan stood at the typewriter in the corner of his room, drinking red wine and smoking and typing away relentlessly for hours."

He was engrossed in writing his next album, an unexpected, controversial fusion of folk and rock created with producer Wilson. The man who had worked on all Dylan's previous albums then predicted things would change for him. "But it wasn't until later that everyone agreed that we should put a band behind him. I had to find a band. But it was a very gradual process." Dylan had first experienced the fusion of folk and rock in the work of John P. Hammond, son of the man who signed him to Columbia, when he was working with three members of The Hawks.

Nonetheless, when Dylan began work on the album on June 13, 1965, it was still as an acoustic artist, playing piano and guitar on ten tracks with Wilson at the controls; however, none was destined to make it on to the new release. The following day, the band Wilson

had assembled – guitarists Al Gorgoni, Kenneth Rankin and Bruce Langhorne, pianist Paul Griffin, bass players Joseph Macho Jnr. and William Lee, plus drummer Bobby Gregg – turned up to play on eight new songs. As usual, they were completed in just a few takes, and included 'Subterranean Homesick Blues', 'Love Minus Zero' and 'She Belongs To Me'.

After a break, Hammond Jnr and The Lovin' Spoonful's John Sebastian joined Langhorne and Dylan in an evening session which produced unacceptable versions of six songs, but the next day it was back on course, with Frank Owens taking over on piano. They worked through tracks including 'Maggie's Farm', 'Gates Of Eden', 'It's All Over Now Baby Blue' and 'Mr. Tambourine Man', although this song, then featuring Ramblin' Jack Elliot, had been taped but rejected in 1964.

The product of three days' recording would be *Bringing It All Back Home* which, despite Dylan recording rock versions of almost every song, appeared in March 1965 with an electric side and a four-song acoustic side featuring Langhorne's balanced guitar accompaniment.

Opener 'Subterranean Homesick Blues' was, for many, the first example of Dylan's move from folk to rock. Written in the New York apartment of his manager's assistant, it tips its hat to Woody Guthrie's 'Taking It Easy' and could be called one of the earliest examples of rap, with its rapid-fire delivery and R&B feel. It would become Dylan's first US chart single, peaking at number 39, and his second UK top 10 hit.

'She Belongs To Me' clearly refers to folk singer, fellow-protester and sometime girlfriend Baez by mentioning an Egyptian ring Dylan had given her. Recorded at the first session on June 13, it was reworked the following day when the electric band assembled in Columbia's Studio B.

'Maggie's Farm' was finished in one take during the final June 15 session; fast-paced and slightly rambling, it also became a UK top 30 hit.

'Love Minus Zero' was one of five songs recorded in three-and-a-half hours with the full band on June 15. Guitarist Langhorne, who also played with Baez, Gordon Lightfoot, Tom Rush and Buffy St Marie, recalled: "We just did first takes … it was amazingly intuitive and successful."

'Mr. Tambourine Man', opening the album's acoustic side, was saved from his previous LP while Dylan perfected it in live performances in the months before these sessions. Written in New Orleans and completed in New Jersey, some consider its lyrics inspired by marijuana while others suggest its title came from the huge tambourine Langhorne played on live dates; recorded by The Byrds, it brought the Los Angeles band a number one hit in both the US and the UK.

This was also the song which introduced a young Mick Hucknall to Bob Dylan. Although he was only five, the leader of Simply Red was impressed by both the song and Dylan's look. "He seemed like the first guy I'd seen just standing there with an acoustic guitar and a mouth organ. 'Mr Tambourine Man' grabbed my attention because of that look but also through the lyrics; I visualized the lyrics and that really captured my imagination."

'It's Alright Ma (I'm Only Bleeding)' was recorded in a single take on the final day of recording and serves as a powerful reminder of Dylan's prowess as a protest singer and his ability to perform 'live' in the studio.

Dylan's fifth studio album closed with fourth acoustic track 'It's All Over Now Baby Blue' inspired, he said, by Gene Vincent's 'Baby Blue' which he sang in his school band days. Seen by some as Dylan's farewell to his earlier self, it earned Baez a UK top 30 hit.

Bringing It All Back Home, featuring Grossman's wife Sally and Dylan's cat Rolling Stone on the cover, became his first US top 10 album and his second UK number one.

Bringing It All Back Home

Released March 1965.
Tracks: Subterranean Homesick Blues, She Belongs To Me, Maggie's Farm, Love Minus Zero, Outlaw Blues, On The Road Again, Bob Dylan's 115th Dream, Mr. Tambourine Man, Gates Of Eden, It's Alright Ma (I'm Only Bleeding), It's All Over Now Baby Blue.

FAR LEFT Sharing a ride with Ramblin' Jack Elliott.

LEFT Dylan offers up a harmonica solo in the studio.

RIGHT One of Dylan's early solo recording sessions in the CBS studios in New York.

Dylan Goes Electric

It was in 1963 when The Beatles first got to grips with the music of Bob Dylan. According to lead guitarist George Harrison, when they embarked on a three-week stint at the Olympia theatre in Paris, "one of the most memorable things for me was that we had a copy of Bob Dylan's *Freewheelin'* album which we played constantly".

John Lennon also recalled the visit to France as pivotal in their exposure to America's newest sensation: "I think that was the first time I ever heard Dylan at all. We all went potty on Dylan."

They met the following year when he visited the group's hotel twice during their second visit to New York in August 1964, and he unquestionably had a profound effect on the songwriting of Lennon and Paul McCartney.

It was in New York's Delmonico Hotel that Dylan also introduced the four boys from Liverpool to marijuana, wrongly believing they were already familiar with the drug; he had misheard the line "I can't hide" in 'I Want To Hold Your Hand' as "I get high." During what Paul described as a "crazy party," Britain's leading group and America's finest singer-songwriter "got on very well and we just talked and had a big laugh," according to Paul.

Lennon later acknowledged that his song 'I'm A Loser' was inspired by Dylan and added, "Anyone who's one of the best in his field – as Dylan is – is bound to influence people. I wouldn't be surprised if we influenced him in some way." In early 1965 Harrison gave his take on the subject of Dylan and The Beatles when he said: "I do know he likes our work and that knocks us out."

While there's no obvious Beatles influence in any of Dylan's songs, he was undoubtedly impressed with their ability and even admitted to being a fan. "It was obvious to me that they had staying power. In my head The Beatles were it," he said, and it's highly likely that they played a part in his decision to 'go electric'.

While it was McCartney who 'discovered' Dylan for The Beatles – he was alerted to Freewheelin' by a French DJ – it seems Lennon was the one most influenced by him.

"'You've Got To Hide Your Love Away' is my Dylan period," he said. "It's one of those you sing a bit sadly to yourself." Others reckoned that the song owed much to 'I Don't Believe In You' from *Another Side Of Bob Dylan*. But it wasn't all mutual back-slapping, as McCartney recalled when he took the band's Sgt *Pepper's Lonely Hearts Club Band* album round to Dylan's hotel room. "I remember playing some of *Sgt Pepper* and he said, 'Oh, I get it – you don't want to be cute any more'."

Whether it was the Beatles who directly influenced Dylan's decision to develop the fusion of folk and rock music and introduce electric guitars and amplification into his recording is something we can never be sure of. According to producer Wilson, who assembled the band on *Bringing It All Back Home*, only one man was

NEWPORT FOLK FESTIVAL

responsible for the move from folk to electric. "It came from me," he told Melody Maker in 1976. For his part, Dylan consistently told reporters that he didn't use an electric guitar "that much at all," before adding: "I just fool around with amplified sometimes."

However, in July 1965 Dylan took his new musical concept out of the studio and on to the road – and the result has gone down in the annals of rock music. At the Newport Folk Festival he was greeted with hostility when, after being introduced by folk singer Pete Yarrow from Peter, Paul and Mary, he walked on stage with a full amplified group, assembled from the Paul Butterfield Blues Band.

In front of the (apparently very loud) five-piece band, Dylan raced through three numbers – 'Maggie's Farm', 'Like A Rolling Stone' and 'Phantom Engineer' (later to appear as 'It Takes A Lot To Laugh, It Takes A Train To Cry') – in what was apparently a spontaneous, unplanned set. Greeted by boos, Dylan left the stage after three numbers, although it's possible they were the only songs the band had rehearsed.

Things were not helped by Dylan's rock-star appearance – black leather jacket, black slacks, a dress shirt and Cuban-heeled boots. The jeering and shouts of "Go back to the Sullivan Show!" seemingly hurt, surprised and upset Dylan, although he did return to the stage with an acoustic guitar, borrowed from Johnny Cash, to perform a solo spot.

Festival director Joe Boyd, later to produce Pink Floyd, The Incredible String Band and Fairport Convention, was not persuaded that the reaction was hostile, suggesting that "More!" and "Boo!" could sound similar when shouted by a huge crowd. "I think it was evenly divided between approbation and condemnation," he insisted.

While a backstage observer commented: "It seems to be one of the few times that Dylan was not in control," the man himself simply said: "It's all music, no more, no less." Four months later Dylan played Hartford, Connecticut, and after a 40-minute acoustic set reappeared with his band for the second half, to be immediately greeted with shouts of "Get rid of the band!" Undeterred, he worked his way through five numbers and, according to a newspaper review, "rocked it up" before leaving the stage, refusing all requests for a post-show interview.

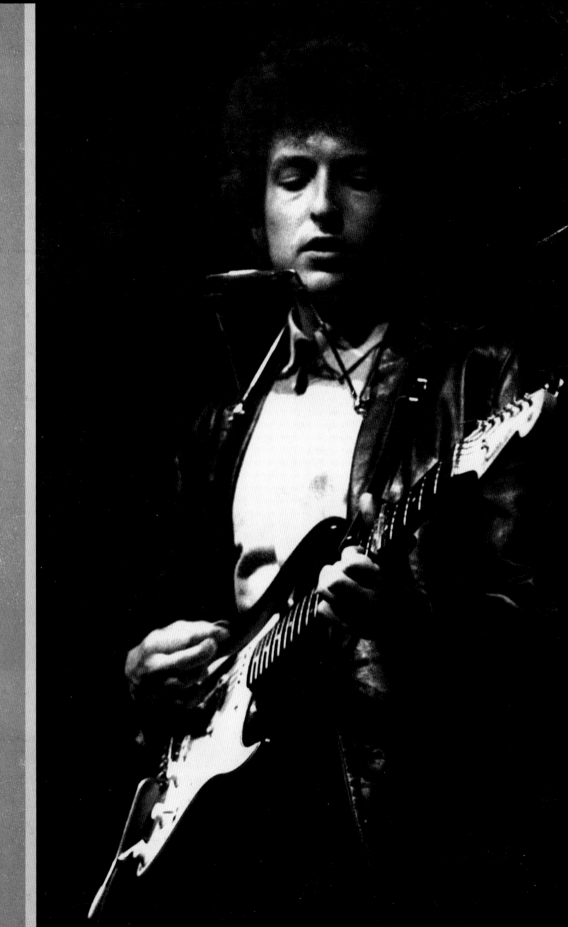

Highway 61 Revisited

Before he embarked on his sixth album during the summer of 1965, Dylan travelled to London to play an eight-date tour filmed by D A Pennebaker as the fly-on-the-wall documentary *Don't Look Back*, released in 1967.

The filming also included what some consider the world's first music video, a sequence shot in an alley behind London's Savoy Hotel with Dylan holding up placards with the lyrics to 'Subterranean Homesick Blues'. During the visit Dylan explained that his still-acoustic show would last for "about an hour and a half," that he hadn't written any songs about Britain ("I didn't write: 'Mrs. Brown You Have A Lovely Cheese'") but that the plane trip had yielded a few ideas ("I made a few notes. I call it stabbing paper.")

Back in New York, Dylan settled back into Columbia's recording studios on Seventh Avenue, and this time he started out with Gregg and Griffin from the *Bringing It All Back Home* sessions, plus lead guitarist Michael Bloomfield and pianist Frank Owens. The sessions, with Wilson still in charge, began on June 15, when three songs were started, and ran on into the next day.

Just four days after his troubled appearance at the Newport Festival, Dylan returned to the studio with the same musicians, but this time without Wilson at the control desk. After working on five albums, he had been replaced by in-house Columbia producer Bob Johnston. He oversaw sessions between July 29 and August 4 when Al Kooper (guitar/organ), Harvey Goldstein (bass), Charlie McCoy (guitar) and Russ Savukus (bass) also arrived in the studio, becoming the first musicians to be credited on a Dylan album.

Altogether nine new Dylan songs were recorded with the new line-up with only one credited to former producer Wilson. This was opening track 'Like A Rolling Stone', a six-minute creation which had taken more than a dozen takes to perfect over the two days in June, with Kooper's first outing on organ making a memorable

ABOVE Captured on film by Donn Pennebaker (in top hat) for the *Don't Look Back* documentary.

RIGHT Another pose for the official photographer in 1967.

contribution to a song that topped *Rolling Stone*'s list of the 500 Greatest Songs Of All Time. Despite its length, it was released as a single and took Dylan into the top five in both the US and UK.

'Ballad Of A Thin Man' was started and completed on August 3 and it seems – despite a claim by Rolling Stone Brian Jones that he was an inspiration, and a suggestion that Joan Baez might even be 'Mr Joans' – that it could well be about *Village Voice* reporter Jeffrey Jones, who claimed he had interviewed and annoyed Dylan backstage at the Newport Festival.

Title track 'Highway 61 Revisited' is Dylan's paean to the main road which ran from his birthplace, Duluth, Minnesota, to the Mississippi Delta, taking in the towns and cities that gave birth to music legends such as Muddy Waters and Elvis Presley; Bessie Smith was killed on the highway and Robert Johnson's famous pact to sell his soul to the devil was supposed to have taken place

at its junction with Highway 49.

Dylan once said: "I always felt like I started on it [*Highway 61*], always had been on it and could go anywhere from it, even down into the deep Delta country," and he was insistent that this would be title of his new album, although he once told biographer Robert Shelton that it had been a fight: "Nobody understood it. I had to go up the fucking ladder until finally the word came down and said, 'Let him call it what he wants to call it'."

The nine-track album – three lasting more than five minutes – finishes with an extraordinary composition which runs out at over 11 minutes and was finally captured on the very last August 4 session. Dubbed by some as Dylan's alternative State of the Union Address, 'Desolation Row' was recorded as an 'electric take' on July 29 before the approved acoustic version – with visiting guitarist McCoy apparently joining Dylan – emerged from a combination of takes 6 and 7.

The album, with a cover photograph credited to Daniel Kramer plus unusual unaccredited shots of Dylan at the piano, ended up being Dylan's first top three album in America and a number four hit in the UK.

In the middle of recording *Highway 61 Revisited*, Dylan also spent

time working on the song 'Positively 4th Street', which took its title from the street he had lived on in Greenwich Village and was an obvious swipe at his former folk friends and fans who sneered at his Newport performance ("You gotta lot of nerve to say you're my friend.") Omitted from the album, it was released as a single and reached the top ten in both the US (number 7) and UK (number 8) in November 1965.

When Mick Hucknall decided to cover Dylan's 'Positively 4th Street' on his 2003 album *Home* he was attracted by one thing in particular. "I loved the lyrics. I like the acerbic, slightly bittersweet thing that he captures in so many of his lyrics. It also struck me as a song that I could do a new arrangement for, different to the one he'd done."

Highway 61 Revisited

Released August 1965. Tracks: Like A Rolling Stone, Tombstone Blues, It Takes A Lot to Laugh, It Takes A Train To Cry, From A Buick 6, Ballad Of A Thin Man, Queen Jane Approximately, Highway 61 Revisited, Just Like Tom Thumb's Blues, Desolation Row.

Enclosures:

item **2** Poster from Bob Dylan's first appearance in New York City, April 11, 1961 at Folk City.

item **3** Flyer from the Wilson High School concert, December 5, 1964.

item **4** Christmas card featuring Dylan photograph, mid-1970s.

item **5** *Don't Look Back* promotional poster, 1967.

item **6** Ticket stub from Bob Dylan and The Band concert at Nassau County Auditorium, NY, January 28, 1974.

item **7** Rolling Thunder Revue poster, 1975–76.

TOP LEFT Dylan takes centre stage with The Byrds at Ciro's club in Los Angeles, California in 1965.

ABOVE Shooting the 'Subterranean Homesick Blues' video in an alley behind London's Savoy Hotel with bearded beat poet Allen Ginsberg.

Blonde On Blonde

After *Highway 61 Revisited* – and before marrying former model Sara Lowndes in November 1965 – Dylan focused his attention on hiring a new touring band. He was now committed to his new music although, interviewed in 1966, he dismissed the idea of musical genres: "As far as folk and folk-rock are concerned, it doesn't matter what kind of nasty name people invent for the music," he told *Playboy*. "I don't think that such a word as folk-rock has anything to do with it." Whatever it was called – and Dylan even suggested "arsenic music" – he needed to find the people to support him.

> **Blonde On Blonde**
>
> Released June 1966. Tracks: Rainy Day Women #12 & 35, Pledging My Time, Visions Of Joanna, One Of Us Must Know (Sooner Or Later), I Want You, Stuck Inside Of Mobile With The Memphis Blues Again, Leopard-Skin Pill-Box Hat, Just Like A Woman, Most Likely You Go Your Way And I'll Go Mine, Temporary Like Achilles, Absolutely Sweet Marie, 4th Time Around, Obviously Believers, Sad Eyed Lady Of The Lowlands.

With Bloomfield and Kooper pulling out, Dylan was searching for musicians to join a mammoth nine-month tour covering the USA, Australia and Europe. He looked to Levon and The Hawks, who had gained recognition in Canada backing Ronnie Hawkins and also worked with John Hammond Jnr.

After a rehearsal in September 1965 and a debut in Austin, Texas, a week later, Dylan travelled to New York with Robbie Robertson (guitar), Rick Danko (bass), Richard Manuel (piano), Garth Hudson (organ) and drummer Levon Helm. They were to be the musicians on his seventh studio album, which he began recording in Columbia's studio on October 5. On November 30 they recorded a new single 'Can You Please Crawl Out Your Window' which was released in December but stalled at number 58 in America and peaked at number 17 in the UK. When Helm left, Gregg and Sandy Kanikoff were used for the remainder of the sessions in December and January.

Dylan and The Hawks in New York was a far from successful combination, and in five days of recording spread over four months only one album track was completed. A downhearted Dylan cancelled future sessions and told critic Robert Shelton: "I was really down. I mean, in ten recording sessions, man, we didn't get one song," presumably forgetting the one they had captured.

At the suggestion of new producer Bob Johnson, and despite manager Grossman's protests, Dylan moved to Columbia's Studio A in Nashville. He took Kooper and Robertson, while local musicians including Charlie McCoy (guitar, bass, harmonica), guitarist Wayne Moss, Joe South (guitar, bass) and drummer Kenny Buttrey

BELOW LEFT, BELOW and RIGHT Fresh from the studio, Dylan took the road with his new band The Hawks in 1966 and played dates in the US, Canada and Europe.

were recruited and even rehearsed, with a piano, in Dylan's hotel room. At the first Nashville session on February 14, 1966, two tracks were recorded, another at an all-nighter the next day and a fourth on the afternoon and evening of February 16.

After taking time out for shows with The Hawks in Canada and the US, Dylan returned to Nashville's famous Music Row in March and in just three days nine tracks were completed, bringing the final tally of album tracks to 14.

Blonde On Blonde was Dylan's first double album, with two songs, 'Visions Of Joanna' and 'Stuck Inside Of Mobile With The Memphis Blues Again', running over seven minutes and another over 11 minutes. Scheduled for release in May, it was delayed until summer and included 'One Of Us Must Know (Sooner Or Later)', the only survivor from the New York sessions.

'Rainy Day Women #12 & 35', with its compulsive refrain "Everybody must get stoned," was completed in one take on the last day in Nashville, and when Johnston suggested: "That sounds like the damn Salvation Army band." Dylan used McCoy on trumpet and local trombone player Wayne Butler to reinforce the feel. As a single, it was a US number two hit, became Dylan's second million-selling single and reached number seven in the UK.

'I Want You' is one of Dylan's most obvious pop songs, with a catchy melody and sing-along chorus, although he manages to mention undertakers, politicians and rock stars along the way; Brian Jones may well be the "dancing child with his Chinese suit". The third single off the album, it reached the Top 20 in both the US and the UK.

'Just Like A Woman' is thought to be about model and actress Edie Sedgwick, part of Andy Warhol's celebrated New York set. It combined what some saw as Dylan's cruellest lyrics with an uplifting melody and was his fourth single of 1966 but failed to make the US top 30 and wasn't released in Britain though Manfred Mann's version was a UK top 10 hit.

The final single from the album, 'Leopard-Skin Pill-Box Hat', was also supposedly inspired by Sedgwick, who some also believe inspired the title *Blonde On Blonde*. Released in April 1967, it just about crept into the US Hot 100.

Dylan's double album – in the days of vinyl – devoted its final side to his epic 'Sad Eyed Lady Of The Lowlands', started and finished overnight on February 15–16 and running for 11 minutes and 23 seconds – too long for most of the musicians, according to drummer Buttrey: "After about ten minutes of this thing we're cracking up at each other. I mean, we peaked five minutes ago."

The lady in the title was the new Mrs Dylan; while he began the song in New York before they were married, he didn't complete it until the day of recording in Nashville.

The *Blonde On Blonde* album made number nine in *Rolling Stone*'s 500 Greatest Albums list and hit the same chart spot in the US, going double platinum; it peaked at number three in the UK and earned Dylan his sixth Top Ten album.

"Judas" The 1966 UK tour

With *Blonde On Blonde* successfully completed and a new band recruited – even if they were more suited to touring than recording – Dylan and The Hawks set off to visit Australia and Europe during the spring of 1966.

As at Newport and throughout the US the year before, the shows were split into two parts. The first half was solo Dylan with his trademark acoustic guitar and harmonica, while the second half involved Dylan and The Hawks playing high-energy, electric rock music.

The confrontation between die-hard folk purists and a broader, more rock-orientated audience was always likely to be volatile, but, once again, it seems that Dylan was not fully prepared for the fallout. It also appeared that he undertook the tour, at the end of a major trek across America, in less than perfect shape. He was worn out, and film-maker Pennebaker recalls that the singer was "taking a lot of amphetamine and who knows what else." Talking to *Rolling Stone* founder Jan Wenner three years after the tour, Dylan admitted: "I was on the road for almost five years. It wore me down."

Exhausted, Dylan arrived in Dublin for shows at the Adelphi Theatre on May 5 and 6 where, during his second-half performance, dozens of people walked out while others assailed him with shouts of "Traitor!" and "Leave it to The Rolling Stones!" Moving from Ireland to England, Dylan once again offered the media a less-than-satisfactory press conference which resulted in accusations that he was rude, arrogant and unco-operative.

New Musical Express writer Keith Altham admitted in his feature that he gave up after a couple of questions, including asking Dylan about singers Paul Simon and Bob Lind. "Never heard of them," was Dylan's reply. At the end of the event the journalist approached one of Dylan's aides – "I knew he was a Dylan man as he had dark glasses on" – and asked why such an obviously intelligent man bothered with such a farcical event. "Dylan just wanted us to come along and record a press reception so we could hear how ridiculous and infantile all reporters are," was the explanation.

However, *Melody Maker*'s Max Jones was luckier, and was treated to a brief one-on-one chat with Dylan in London. The music journalist asked Dylan if he was going to use an amplified guitar during his UK shows and was told: "I'm not sure if I will or not." Pressed further on the subject of protest songs, the American singer explained: "All my songs are protest songs. All I do is protest. You name it, I'll protest about it."

During shows in Bristol, Birmingham and Leicester there were more whistles and cat-calls during the second-half performances before the now legendary concert at Manchester's Free Trade Hall on May 17. Here a student, later identified as Keith Butler, was famously captured on tape shouting "Judas!" at Dylan. The singer replied: "I don't believe you," before adding: "You're a liar," and urging his band "to play fuckin' loud" as they launched into their closing number, 'Like A Rolling Stone'.

The European leg of Dylan's tour ended at London's Royal Albert Hall with shows on May 26 and 27 and, despite The Beatles and The Rolling Stones being in the hall, there were mass walkouts and heckling. While George Harrison suggested that the protesters were "idiots", the reviewers were less than impressed, with Melody Maker's Ray Coleman describing the show as a shambles and The Daily Telegraph tagging Dylan as a performer "who does not care whether he communicates or not."

Speaking from the stage during the second half of his show on Friday, May 27, Dylan told the crowd: "I like my old songs. It's just that things change all the time." He went on to explain: "We've been playing this music since we were ten years old. Folk music was just an interruption and was very useful. If you don't like it (the new songs), that's fine."

After the show John Lennon and Paul McCartney made it back to Dylan's hotel suite where Lennon reportedly told the singer: "Best bloody show I've ever seen, Bob." The Rolling Stones also went along to the after-show event to meet Dylan, although Keith Richards, by his own admission, was "pretty frightened of him," while it seems Dylan was less than impressed by the songs The Stones wrote, as he told the band's lead guitarist: "I could write 'Satisfaction', but you couldn't write 'Mr Tambourine Man'."

Having announced on stage: "I'm not going to play any more concerts in England," Dylan left the UK and departed for a brief holiday in Spain before returning to New York to look at rushes of the documentary film *Don't Look Back*. On July 29, two months after his last London date, Dylan crashed his Triumph Bonneville 650 motorcycle near his home in Woodstock and reportedly suffered a broken neck vertebra. Few details have ever emerged about the crash or Dylan's injuries, but there's no doubt it came at a time when Dylan needed to ease up and take stock of his career and his life. "I was pretty wound up before the accident happened. I probably would have died if I'd kept on going the way I had been" was Dylan's own assessment of his situation in 1966.

LEFT An exhausted Dylan hit the UK in May 1966.   **ABOVE** Dylan heard the fans shout "traitor" and "Judas", but still played on in 1966.

John Wesley Harding

Whether he was recovering from the injuries sustained in his motorcycle accident or simply recuperating from a gruelling five years of touring and recording, Bob Dylan disappeared from the public gaze for more than 12 months during 1966 and 1967.

Rumours circulated that he was spending time in his Woodstock home working on a novel – he had signed a lucrative publishing deal some years earlier – in addition to pursuing his new interest in painting. He was also being a father to Sara's five-year-old daughter Maria and preparing for the birth of their son Jesse.

Either way, it was assumed that he wasn't actively pursuing his musical career, although it later transpired that The Hawks were busy in a studio they had set up in a rented house in Woodstock known as the Big Pink. Dylan was a regular visitor to the house, which was painted the colour of a strawberry milkshake, and during 1967 they recorded more than 100 songs together. "We were doing seven, eight … sometimes 15 songs a day," said the band's keyboard player Garth Hudson. These sessions inspired The Hawks to reappear as The Band and release their hugely successful debut album Music From The Big Pink.

Other recordings from the session turned up later on Dylan's 1975 album *The Basement Tapes*, while acts as diverse as Manfred Mann ('The Mighty Quinn'), Peter, Paul and Mary ('Too Much Of Nothing'), The Byrds ('You Ain't Goin' Nowhere') and Julie Driscoll, Brian Auger and The Trinity ('This Wheel's On Fire') all had hits with Dylan songs during 1968.

While fans had to make do with the 1967 release of a first *Greatest Hits* collection, which was a top ten hit in both America and Britain, Dylan signed a new and much improved recording deal with Columbia – his royalty was upped to ten per cent – in July 1967 and returned to the studio four months later.

Despite his sessions in Woodstock, Dylan decided to start afresh and once again travelled to Nashville to begin recording on October 17, 1967, with Bob Johnston back on the desk. He had a new set of songs but, according to The Band's Robbie Robertson, went to Tennessee "on a kind of whim" to record once again with drummer Kenny Buttrey and bassist Charlie McCoy, plus pedal steel guitarist Pete Drake.

Johnston recalled that Dylan first played him the songs he had in mind to record in his Nashville hotel room and "suggested that we should just use bass and guitar and drums on the record.

I said 'Fine', but also suggested we add a steel guitar." The whole album was completed in just three days of recording – October 17, November 6 and November 29 – and John Wesley Harding was released in the last week of December 1967, a turnaround of less than four weeks after the final sessions.

Although he returned to a more acoustic style, Dylan's stark and even austere presentation of his songs may have resulted from Woody Guthrie's death in September 1966, just a couple of weeks before recording began.

Talking to *Rolling Stone* magazine in 1969, Dylan explained the reasoning behind the album's title. "I called it that because I had that song 'John Wesley Harding'. It fits right in tempo. I was gonna

ABOVE Dylan offers his best side to the photographers.

LEFT The Hawks came from Canada and became bestsellers as The Band.

RIGHT Dylan and The Band remember Woody Guthrie at a New York memorial concert in 1968.

John Wesley Harding

Released 1967. Tracks: John Wesley Harding, As I Went Out One Morning, I Dreamed I Saw St Augustine, All Along The Watchtower, The Ballad Of Frankie Lee and Judas Priest, Drifters Escape, Dear Landlord, I Am A Lonesome Hobo, I Pity The Poor Immigrant, The Wicker Messenger, Down Along The Cove, I'll Be Your Baby Tonight.

write a ballad … a real long ballad. But in the middle of the second verse I got tired."

The album's title track was in fact completed on November 6, and tells of an American outlaw and gunfighter who was shot and killed in Texas in 1895.

'I'll Be Your Baby Tonight' is an up-tempo, country-flavoured, odd-ball love song which Dylan finished in the final three hours of the last day of recording.

The album's stand-out track 'All Along The Watchtower' also came from the second session in the first week of November and Dylan's album version differs from the live version he has offered up since 1970. The turning point was Jimi Hendrix's hard rock cover version which reached number 20 in the US and was a Top Five hit in the UK in 1968, two years before his death. Dylan explained, "I like Jimi Hendrix's record and ever since he died I've been doing it that way. When I sing I always feel it's a tribute to him in some kind of way."

At Dylan's insistence, John Wesley Harding was released with the minimum of promotion and publicity during the commercially 'dead' Christmas holiday period but it still managed to hit the number two spot in America and top the UK charts for a period of 13 weeks during 1968.

A week after the album's release Dylan returned to the stage for the first time since 1966 when he joined The Band at New York's Carnegie Hall for a concert in memory of Woody Guthrie.

Nashville Skyline

Following the enormous and even surprising success of *John Wesley Harding*, particularly in the light of Dylan's best efforts to under-promote the album, the singer spent much of 1969 concerned about his privacy ... or lack of it.

He had experienced intruders invading his property and suffered the displeasure of his neighbours – "To them it must've seemed I was something out of a carnival show," he commented – while the media continued to push him forward as a generation's spokesman. "I wasn't the toastmaster of a generation," was Dylan's reply to these assertions.

Nevertheless, he returned to Nashville in February 1969 to begin work on his ninth studio album, more than a year after his last recording sessions in 1967, and now he was intent on dipping into a new well of inspiration as he enveloped himself in the music America's southern states knew best – country.

He approached the sessions for Nashville Skyline with a collection of songs which, in his own words, were "easy to understand and there ain't too many words to remember." Once again Buttrey, McCoy and Drake were on hand to help out established producer Johnston and this time they were all joined by Bob Wilson (piano) and guitarists Norman Blake and Charlie Daniels.

Dylan and his half-dozen country players rattled through three tracks on February 13, four more on the following day and a further two on February 17. Explaining the rapid and easy-going studio work, Dylan recalled: "We just take a song, play it and everyone else just sort of fills in behind it. At the same time ... there's someone in the control booth who's turning all the dials to where the proper sound is coming in." Throughout these sessions it was also apparent to everyone involved that Dylan had discovered a new, smooth, country-crooner singing voice which the man himself attributed to a break from smoking.

While Dylan was in Columbia's Nashville studio complex another major star was in the next studio, and pretty soon Dylan was working with Johnny Cash. During the final February 17 session they recorded three songs, but the next day they ran through a further 15 including 'That's Alright Mama', 'Mystery Train', 'I Walk The Line', 'Ring Of Fire', 'You Are My Sunshine' and 'Just A Closer Walk With Thee'. Ultimately all these duets were rejected, until it came to a song that had first appeared on *The Freewheelin' Bob Dylan* album six years earlier.

'Girl From The North Country' was one of the last songs Dylan and Cash recorded together in Nashville, and Dylan chose it as the opening track of his new album. Later, they also sang it on Cash's TV show, while Cash added his own personal and poetic liner notes to

Nashville Skyline
Released April 1969.
Tracks: Girl From The North Country, Nashville Skyline Rag, To Be Alone With You, Threw It All Away, Peggy Day, Lay Lady Lay, One More Night, Tell Me That It Isn't True, Country Pie, Tonight I'll Be Staying Here With You.

LEFT A bespectacled Dylan takes a ride in the country.

RIGHT The quaint good ol' boy look Dylan adopted for the cover of *Nashville Skyline*.

the album: "This man can rhyme the track of time. The edge of pain, the what of sane." In 1969 Cash received a Grammy Award for Best Album Notes for his effort.

While 'Peggy Day' and 'One More Night' were dismissed as frivolous and the instrumental 'Nashville Skyline Rag' as unimportant, the whole of *Nashville Skyline* (which consisted of just ten tracks and lasted only 27 minutes) was condemned in some quarters as "routine" and "slight." Two singles were released from the album, 'I Threw It All Away' and 'Tonight I'll Be Staying Here With You', but both failed to get into the top 30 in either America or the UK.

However, there was one track which impressed critics and fans alike. 'Lay Lady Lay', completed on February 14, had been composed as a possible theme song for the film *Midnight Cowboy* but missed the deadline. Dylan later offered it to the Everly Brothers, only to have it rejected, and he then decided to record it himself. However, once it was

finished, he "begged and pleaded" with Columbia's bosses not to issue it as a single, explaining, "I was slightly embarrassed by it. I wasn't even sure I ever liked the song." In the end the label was proved right, as 'Lay Lady Lay' became Dylan's first top ten hit for three years – reaching number seven in the US and number five in the UK.

Bizarrely, *Nashville Skyline* was at one time set to be called John *Wesley Harding Volume II* or *Tonight I'll Be Staying Here With Peggy Day* and even *Peggy Day – Lay, Peggy Day*. "A lot of things were brought up. Some of the names just didn't seem to fit," Dylan confirmed. Eventually it peaked at number three in America and became his fourth UK number one album: but, perhaps more importantly, *Nashville Skyline* – despite its slightly strange country-bumpkin cover photograph of Dylan – introduced country music to a wider, more mainstream audience and opened the way for a host of new country rock artists.

Isle of Wight Festival 1969

Three years after he had suffered booing and heckling during concerts on his British tour, Dylan surprised almost everyone and returned to the United Kingdom to play a one-off concert in front of nearly 200,000 people on a small island located around three miles off England's south coast.

After his 1966 tour, when he introduced The Band and his 'new' electric sound to stunned audiences, and his motorcycle accident later the same year, *Melody Maker*'s respected folk writer Karl Dallas had predicted: "Bob Dylan is unlikely ever to appear in concert again," and when the singer turned down the opportunity to play in his own backyard at the inaugural Woodstock Festival in New York State in August 1969, it looked as though Dylan's career as a live performer might genuinely have come to an end.

Although the Woodstock site in Bethel was actually 60 miles away from his home in neighbouring Byrdcliffe, Dylan wasn't impressed with the idea of thousands of music fans rampaging around the area. After the four-day festival, which ran from August

15 to 18, he said, "It seemed to have something to do with me, this Woodstock nation and everything it represented. So we couldn't breathe. I couldn't get any space for me and my family."

While it was rumoured that the festival organizers had deliberately chosen Woodstock in an effort to persuade Dylan to come out of retirement, the plan backfired when he upped sticks and instead opted to perform at a festival which the year before had attracted 10,000 and been held on a farm to raise funds for a swimming pool.

Paid an impressive £50,000, Dylan flew first-class from America with his family and The Band for the second Isle of Wight festival, taking place in the village of Wootton over the August Bank

LEFT A smiling Dylan at the Isle of Wight festival.

RIGHT Relaxing by the sea during a British bank holiday.

Holiday weekend. This time, the thousands of fans paid either £2.10s (£2.50p) for a two-day pass or just £2 for a Sunday-only ticket and were entertained by the likes of The Moody Blues, Joe Cocker, Free, Tom Paxton, Pentangle and The Who, who closed Saturday's festivities.

During his brief stay on the island, famous for Parkhurst Prison and Queen Victoria's country residence of Osborne House, Dylan ensconced himself at Fernlands Farm and stayed pretty much out of sight, although he did appear at a brief press conference when he confirmed that it was "great to be here," and explained: "I don't want to protest any more" and outlined his set list with the words, "Everything we will do is on record."

While a number of the other acts included Dylan songs in their performances, the big Isle of Wight rumour was that George Harrison, The Rolling Stones and Blind Faith would join Dylan and his band on stage for an almighty jam session. In the end they all satisfied themselves by staying close to the stage and eventually watching Bob Dylan's very late, and very brief, return to the stage

to top the bill on Sunday, August 30.

Two hours later than scheduled, he eventually went on stage at 11pm – explaining: "I was here at 5.30, ready to go on, but I was kept waiting until 11pm" – and surprised everyone by appearing with his hair neatly trimmed and dressed incongruously in a white suit.

During his disappointingly short set, Dylan ran through 17 songs, beginning with 'She Belongs To Me' and moving on to the hugely popular collection of 'Maggie's Farm', 'Mr. Tambourine Man', 'Lay Lady Lay', 'Like a Rolling Stone' and 'The Mighty Quinn' before closing with 'Rainy Day Women #12 & 35'. His explanation was simple. "I played long enough. I didn't want to go on much longer."

Melody Maker's reviewer described Dylan's performance as "a programme of mainly familiar Dylan compositions but in new vocal and instrumental settings. His voice sounded confident, well in tune and free of the old harshness." It was suggested that around 300 American journalists and broadcasters made their

way to the Isle of Wight for Dylan's return to the stage – no doubt disappointed by his non-appearance at their homeland Woodstock event.

Also in the crowd which assembled in a field on a farm was Apple Records executive Tony Bramwell, who travelled down with Eric Clapton, Jack Bruce and Ginger Baker from Cream especially to see Dylan. "We bussed into the backstage area just before Bob went on and watched his set from six feet in front of the stage," he said, before adding, "None of us was very impressed, so we got back on the bus and were back in London by one in the morning."

There's no doubt that Dylan's return to the stage disappointed those who had anticipated a three-hour show with a possible all-star finale, and the singer himself may been equally downhearted by the way things turned out. Before the festival he had spoken of his appearance as a comeback, but these plans were hastily shelved along with the idea of a live album recording of his long-awaited, over-hyped return. As the *New Musical Express* critic said, "The crowd obviously expected more but they didn't get it."

ABOVE After three years away, Dylan returned to the UK to play his late, late festival show behind a bank of microphones.

Self Portrait and New Morning

Ever enigmatic, Dylan moved on from his serious collection of country rock songs on *Nashville Skyline* to produce a double album which, although it failed to impress the critics, did continue his run of commercial successes.

He called *Self Portrait* "a bunch of tracks that we'd done all the time I'd gone to Nashville. And then there was a lot of stuff that was just on the shelf." With Johnston again in charge, the sessions in Nashville and New York spanned nearly a year, from April 1969 to March 1970.

The result was Dylan's second double album, which featured around 50 musicians on two dozen tracks. Besides regulars Buttrey, McCoy, Drake and Kooper, there were all five of The Band plus string and horn sections, while the songs ranged from classics such as 'Blue Moon' and American backwoods song 'Copper Kettle' to live versions of 'Like A Rolling Stone', 'The Mighty Quinn' and 'She Belongs To Me', recorded live at the Isle of Wight.

Released in June 1970, it featured the country crooning voice Dylan had used earlier but this time strings, horns and a small choir were generously overdubbed. Some critics were savage – Greil Marcus' review in *Rolling Stone* opened with the line: "What is this shit?" – and Dylan seemed to acknowledge *Self Portrait* was a sub-standard offering, maybe even made as a joke and released "to get people off my back". However, it had at least one big fan – The

Who's Pete Townshend who said "It was a bit of a dip-in-and-see record, lots of different styles, and I was inspired by it. I thought, 'This guy is a great genius, no question about it'."

As to why it was a double album, Dylan bizarrely explained: "Well, it wouldn't have held up as a single album – then it really would've been bad. I mean if you're gonna put a lot of crap on it, you might as well load it up." Speaking in 1985, he went further and said: "I just figured I'd put all this stuff together and put it out: my own bootleg, so to speak."

Critics notwithstanding, it still reached number four in the US and was Dylan's third successive UK number one album. It also came with unique cover artwork. "I did this self-portrait for the cover," said Dylan. "I mean, there was no title for the album. I knew somebody who had some paints and a square canvas and I did the cover in about five minutes. And I said I'm gonna call the album *Self Portrait*."

Within five months of the release of his much-criticized double album, Dylan had issued a new LP, perhaps in an effort to reduce the damage done by *Self Portrait*.

Recorded in New York between June and August 1970, *New Morning* consisted of 12 new songs and marked the return of Dylan's familiar nasal singing voice. It was also apparent that many of the songs already existed when *Self Portrait* came out, although Dylan denied rushing the album out following criticism of his earlier effort. "It wasn't like that. It just happened coincidentally that one came out and then the other one did as soon as it did. We were working on *New Morning* when the *Self Portrait* album got put together."

In fact, during sessions for the earlier album Dylan began recording songs that would eventually appear on *New Morning*, although they were re-worked before inclusion. Among the musicians who joined him for the *New Morning* sessions on May 1, 1970, were George Harrison, Charlie Daniels and drummer Russ Kunkel.

In spring 1970 Dylan agreed to provide songs for poet Archibald MacLeish's play, *Scratch*, and duly created 'New Morning', 'Times Passes Slowly' and 'Father Of The Night'. However, following a

LEFT Bob Dylan & Johnny Cash duet on TV.

ABOVE On stage in Los Angeles at the 1970 Woody Guthrie memorial show.

RIGHT George Harrison and Dylan performing in New York during the 1971 Concert for Bangla Desh at Madison Square Garden.

Self Portrait

Released 1970. Tracks: All The Tired Horses, Alberta #1, I Forgot More Than You'll Ever Know, Days Of 49, Early Morning Rain, In Search Of Little Sadie, Let It Be Me, Little Sadie, Woogieboogie, Belle Isle, Living The Blues, Like A Rolling Stone, Copper Kettle, I Gotta Travel On, Blue Moon, The Boxer, Quinn The Eskimo, Take Me As I Am, Take A Message To Mary, It Hurts Me Too, Minstrel Boy, She Belongs To Me, Wigwam, Alberta #2.

dispute with the producer he withdrew his songs from the play but included them on his new album.

From June 1 to 5, ensconced in Columbia's Studio E, Dylan completed most of the work for his album. Sessions on July 13 and 23 yielded some rejected efforts but on August 12 Dylan finally completed the last tracks for *New Morning* in the company of Kooper. He had taken over as producer from Johnston who, it seems, departed some time in July, leaving Kooper to deal with Dylan's demands. "When I finished the album I never wanted to speak to him again", commented Kooper. "He changed his mind every three

seconds so I ended up doing the work of three albums."

The song 'Went To See The Gypsy' chronicles a supposed get-together between Dylan and Elvis Presley, though there's no hard evidence they ever met. Dylan did, however, go to see him at Madison Square Garden in 1972, two years after recording this song.

'If Not For You' is one of Dylan's more uplifting love songs and again features Kooper's distinctive organ-playing. A duet with George Harrison was recorded but not included on the album (although Harrison featured it on his *All Things Must Pass* album) and it was left to Olivia Newton-John to release it as her debut chart single in 1971.

New Morning took Dylan's tally of UK number one albums to six – four in succession – and while it peaked at number seven in the US, it did become his eighth top ten album in seven years.

New Morning
Released 1970. Tracks: If Not For You, Day Of The Locusts, Time Passes Slowly, Went To See The Gypsy, Winterlude, If Dogs Run Free, New Morning, Sign On The Window, One More Weekend, The Man In Me, Three Angels, Father Of the Night.

Dylan at the Movies

Bob Dylan's first involvement with the film *Pat Garrett And Billy The Kid* came in late 1972 when he was sent the screenplay by writer Rudy Wurlitzer with an invitation to write a couple of songs for the soundtrack.

Immediately attracted by the idea of actually having a role in the film, Dylan travelled to Mexico to meet director Sam Peckinpah, a man apparently completely unaware of Dylan's standing as a rock musician. However, when Dylan played him the song 'Billy', he was moved to offer him a part as 'Alias', a member of the outlaw gang.

Working alongside James Coburn as Sheriff Pat Garrett and Kris Kristofferson as Billy the Kid, Dylan worked in Durango, Mexico, from late 1972 until early 1973 – with a break for Christmas – but found his role being slowly reduced as Peckinpah grew more unstable and irascible. "There I was, trapped deep in the heart

of Mexico. With some madman," was the singer's assessment of his movie debut. While his role drew a favourable response from Kristofferson – "You see him on the screen and all eyes are on him. There's something about him that's magnetic" – the critics were less impressed, one describing his acting as "an assortment of tics, smirks, winks, shrugs and smiles."

The first session for the soundtrack album took place in the CBS Discos studios in Mexico City on January 20, when 'Billy 7' was successfully recorded, before Dylan moved to work in the Burbank studios in Los Angeles in February, where he completed the remaining nine tracks including the stand-out song chosen as

his new single. While the album hit the top 20 in America and the top 30 in the UK, 'Knockin' On Heaven's Door' became his best-selling single for four years and has been successfully covered by both Eric Clapton and Guns N' Roses.

Having been passed over for the role of Woody Guthrie in the film *Bound For Glory* (the part went to David Carradine), Dylan opted to make his own movie in 1975. His *Rolling Thunder* touring revue provided the setting for *Renaldo And Clara*, which Dylan directed, co-wrote with Sam Shepherd and starred in alongside his wife Sara, ex-girlfriend Joan Baez, singer Ronnie Hawkins (who appears as Bob Dylan) and poet Allen Ginsberg, plus Harry Dean

ABOVE Dylan's white-faced image from *Renaldo and Clara*.　　**RIGHT** As 'Alias' in *Pat Garret and Billy The Kid*.

Stanton, who appeared in Pat Garrett.

As there was no discernible plot, the film – which ran for nearly four hours – ended up as part-documentary and part-improvization with narrative-free passages, scenes of concert performances and footage of singers Phil Ochs and David Blue, plus boxer Rubin Carter. After its initial showing in 1978, when it was savaged by the critics, Dylan created a shorter two-hour version but eventually he withdrew the film from circulation.

Almost a decade after *Renaldo And Clara*, Dylan returned to the big screen to play rock legend- turned-chicken farmer Billy Parker in *Hearts Of Fire*, directed by Richard Marquand (famous for *Return of the Jedi* and *Jagged Edge*) and starring Fiona Flanagan as Dylan's love interest and Englishman Rupert Everett as a rival, youthful rock star. Even though he contributed two songs – 'Had A Dream About You Baby' and 'Night After Night' – plus cover versions of 'The Usual' and 'Couple More Years', the majority of the music was created by composer John Barry. Filmed in Canada, England and Wales, with concert footage shot in Bristol's Colston Hall and in Camden, London, *Hearts Of Fire* was released in 1987 to such poor reviews that it was withdrawn from the UK cinema circuit after just two weeks and never released to theatres in America.

Having played a rock star in one film, Dylan did it again in 2003, appearing as Jack Fate in the 'comedy-drama' *Masked And Anonymous*, directed by Larry Charles, the successful writer of TV's *Seinfeld* and *Mad About You*.

With a stellar cast including John Goodman, Jeff Bridges, Penelope Cruz, Val Kilmer, Mickey Rourke and Jessica Lange – plus a script co-written by Dylan, under the alias Sergei Petrov – the film is set around 'Fate' being released from prison to play a one-man benefit concert to help the victims of a rapidly decaying American society.

The music was supplied by Dylan and his regular touring band of Charlie Sexton, Larry Campbell, Tony Garnier and George Receli, who appear as Fate's backing band Simple Twist Of Fate; between them they perform versions of 'Blowin' In the Wind', 'Dirt Road Blues', 'Not Dark Yet' and 'A Hard Rain's Gonna Fall'.

Shot in just three weeks for around $7 million – some of the cast worked for the union rate in order to appear with Dylan – *Masked And Anonymous* was launched at the 2003 Sundance Film Festival, where it was reviewed as "a vanity production beyond reason." As a result of the poor reaction, the film was denied a theatrical release in the UK.

LEFT Playing the rock star Billy Parker in *Heart of Fire*.

ABOVE In costume and on the set for *Masked And Anonymous*.

Planet Waves and Before The Flood

The end of the 1960s also saw Bob Dylan bring the curtain down on two long relationships in his professional career as a musician.

When his contract with manager Albert Grossman came up for renewal around the time of the Woodstock Festival, Dylan decided it was time he took charge of his own affairs with the help of advisers. This meant that it was very much his own decision to leave Columbia Records when his contract with the label he joined in 1962 came up for renewal in 1973.

The prospect of Bob Dylan being a free agent brought out the music industry's big guns, as almost every major label went after the million-selling singer-songwriter. At the front of the queue was David Geffen, who had founded Asylum Records in 1972 after a period co-managing Joni Mitchell, Jackson Browne and Crosby, Stills and Nash.

So determined was Geffen to sign Dylan that he courted his friend Robbie Robertson, from The Band, and even held meetings with Dylan on the beach near the singer's home in Malibu, California. Eventually Geffen got his man to sign to his Asylum label, his plan being not only to release Dylan's records but also to get him back on the road with The Band.

The first Asylum album came about following rehearsals with The Band in Malibu, which prompted Dylan to head for New York in October 1973 to compose new material. By the time he returned and went into the Village Recorders studio in Los Angeles in November, he had nine new songs. Between November 2 and 14, under the direction of producer/engineer Rob Fraboni, Dylan and The Band then completed the new album, which had the working title *Ceremonies Of The Horsemen*. The first, and only, studio album

Planet Waves

Released 1974. Tracks: On A Night Like This, Going Going Gone, Tough Mama, Hazel, Something There Is About You, Forever Young, Dirge, You Angel You, Never Say Goodbye, Wedding Song.

ABOVE Dylan returned to the stage to tour America in 1974.
RIGHT A poster for his 1974 tour with The Band.
OPPOSITE LEFT Ten shows were recorded for a live album.
OPPOSITE RIGHT The Band's Rick Danko and Robbie Robertson with Dylan.

Before The Flood

Released 1975. Tracks: Most Likely You Go Your Way (And I'll Go Mine), Lay Lady Lay, Rainy Day Women #12 & 35, Knockin' On Heaven's Door, It Ain't Me Babe, Ballad Of A Thin Man, Up On Cripple Creek, I Shall Be Released, Endless Highway, The Night They Drove Old Dixie Down, Stage Fright, Don't Think Twice It's Alright, Just Like A Woman, It's Alright Ma, The Shape I'm In, When You Awake, The Weight, All Along The Watchtower, Highway 61 Revisited, Like A Rolling Stone, Blowin' In the Wind.

Dylan ever recorded with The Band was particularly memorable for Fraboni who said: "It was striking to do something that powerful that quickly." Closing track 'Wedding Song' is an example of how rapidly things happened; Dylan wrote it lying on the floor of the control room and then recorded it in one take on November 9. 'Forever Young', on the other hand, was started – without

drummer Levon Helm, who was still making his way to California – on November 4, attempted again on November 5 and then on November 8, 9 and 14. Dylan told Fraboni: "I been carrying this song around in my head for five years and I never wrote it down and now I come to record it, I just can't decide how to do it." In the end two different master takes from two separate sessions were included on the album, now retitled *Planet Waves*.

Once again the album's artwork was a painting by Dylan and it contains the words 'Cast-Iron Songs And Torch Ballads' plus a Campaign for Nuclear Disarmament (CND) symbol. *Planet Waves* came out on the Island label in the UK, where it reached number seven, while his only studio album for Asylum would finally see Bob Dylan reach number one in the US … and stay there for five weeks.

Back on the road for the first time since his 1966 tour, Bob Dylan took The Band on a 39-date tour of America in January 1974 and the public's response was overwhelming – with more than five million applications for a total of 660,000 tickets. But according to Melody Maker's man in New York, who saw a Thursday afternoon show in Madison Square Garden, the only words Dylan spoke

during the show were "Back in ten minutes" when it came to the half-time interval.

Ahead of the tour, Dylan and his label Asylum decided on a spread of ten separate live recordings in venues around the country – three at Madison Square Garden in New York, two at Seattle's Center Coliseum, two more in Oakland's Alameda County Coliseum and three at the Los Angeles Forum.

In the event, the double album *Before The Flood* consisted of 20 tracks recorded in Los Angeles, plus one song – 'Knockin' On Heaven's Door' – from New York, and also included eight songs by The Band, including 'Up On Cripple Creek', 'Stage Fright' and 'The Weight'. While some classic Dylan songs were missing, there were impressive versions of 'All Along The Watchtower', 'Like A Rolling Stone' and 'Lay Lady Lay' plus a brief acoustic set featuring 'Don't Think Twice It's Alright', 'Just Like A Woman' and 'It's Alright Ma'. Some have suggested the album's title refers to the idea of releasing the official live album before the inevitable flood of bootlegs.

Before The Flood was a number three hit in America and reached number eight in the UK.

Blood On The Tracks and The Rolling Thunder Revue

Dylan's return to live work in 1974 profoundly affected the life of domestic bliss he had seemingly been living since his marriage to Sara in 1965. He was thrown back into life on the road and soon discovered it could be enjoyable and inspirational. By the time the tour was over, he was involved with record executive Ellen Bernstein and separated from his wife.

Back in New York, Dylan revisited his old Greenwich Village haunts and even began to take painting classes before returning to his Minnesota farm to begin the songs for his next album.

Having re-signed with Columbia, where Bernstein worked, Dylan moved into the old Columbia studios in New York, now renamed A&R Studios, with Phil Ramone acting as engineer to Dylan the producer. "Never turning off the tape machine was part of the way you recorded Dylan," explained Ramone.

Banjo player Eric Weissberg and his band Deliverance were hired, and quickly fired, to be replaced by bass player Tony Brown, organist Paul Griffin and steel guitarist Buddy Cage for sessions that ran from September 16 to 19. During those three days Dylan recorded, mixed and even cut a test pressing of the new album which Columbia was all set to release, until Dylan returned to the Sound 80 Studios in Minnesota in December.

Here, in three days immediately following Christmas, Dylan re-recorded six songs with a selection of local players and rewrote some lyrics during time with his children and brother. *Blood On The Tracks* was released in January 1975 with ten tracks and a strange, mottled, profile shot of Dylan on the cover.

Opening track 'Tangled Up In Blue' is a long, narrative work which some have called his finest song. While he once said it took him "ten years to love and two years to write," it was in fact written during time spent on his Minnesota farm without his wife in 1974. On the other hand, 'You're Gonna Make Me Lonesome When You Go' is about the other woman in his life, Ellen Bernstein, and seemingly continues the album's themes of loneliness, sorrow and anger.

'Idiot Wind' – at just under eight minutes – was finished in New York and then dramatically altered when Dylan got to Minnesota, where he made it more personal and arguably even more bitter. While Dylan's son Jakob once claimed the songs on *Blood On The Tracks* "are my parents talking," Dylan himself remarked to his old friend Mary Travers (from Peter, Paul and Mary): "A lot of people told me they enjoyed that album. It's hard for me to relate to that … people enjoying that type of pain."

Painful and personal as it may have been, *Blood On The Tracks*, after receiving less than impressive initial reviews, has since been acknowledged as one of Dylan's greatest works, *Daily Telegraph* writer Neil McCormick suggested it's "the most intricate, eloquent and savagely remorseless examination of the downside of love ever committed to record."

The album, described by Ramone as "a major turnaround" in Dylan's life, became his second successive US number one and peaked at number four in the UK, though single 'Tangled Up In Blue' stalled at number 31 in the US.

ABOVE The Rolling Thunder Revue kicked off in October 1975.

LEFT On stage at a San Francisco benefit in March 1975.

RIGHT Dylan (second from right) on stage with (L to R) Richie Havens, Joan Baez and Ramblin' Jack Elliott.

Blood On The Tracks

Released 1975. Tracks: Tangled Up in Blue, Simple Twist Of Fate, You're A Big Girl Now, Idiot Wind, You're Gonna Make Me Lonesome When You Go, Meet Me In the Morning, Lily Rosemary and Jack Of Hearts, If You See Her Say Hello, Shelter From The Storm, Buckets Of Rain.

Having toured America in 1974, Dylan embarked on a new concept in touring in late 1975 with the Rolling Thunder Revue, featuring the likes of Baez, Roger McGuinn, Joni Mitchell, Allen Ginsberg, David Blue and Ramblin' Jack Elliott as walk-on guests in a giant travelling circus.

Also recruited for the two legs of the Rolling Thunder Revue – named, it seems, either after a Native American shaman, America's Vietnam bombing campaign or Dylan's own suggestion that he heard

"Boom, boom, boom, boom rolling from west to east" – was English guitarist Mick Ronson. Previously one of David Bowie's Spiders From Mars, he recalled Dylan phoned him two days before rehearsals began and asked: "Would I be there?" After touring the US between October and December 1974 and again in April and May 1976, Ronson said: "The whole thing was an adventure, a treasure hunt." Part of Dylan's thinking, he said, was "to embark upon the New England dates to celebrate in some way America's bicentennial year".

He also confirmed: "He doesn't talk much at all. He's just around and you know he's there. He doesn't have to say anything."

The Rolling Thunder Revue closed its first run with a major show at Madison Square Garden on December 8, a benefit for boxer Rubin 'Hurricane' Carter, whom many believed to have been wrongfully convicted of murder. The show, Night Of The Hurricane, was hosted by Muhammed Ali and also featured Roberta Flack.

Desire, Hard Rain and Street Legal

Before embarking on his Rolling Thunder Revue, Dylan began work on a new album, this time with a co-writer. Jacques Levy had collaborated with Roger McGuinn to create The Byrds' hit 'Chestnut Mare', and a meeting with Dylan in Greenwich Village sparked a friendship which resulted in Dylan asking him to write some material for him.

On July 14, 1975, in Columbia's New York studio, Dylan finally began work on the first songs he and Levy had created, 'Joey', an epic ballad about the gangster Joey Gallo, and 'Rita Mae', a short song about Rita Mae Brown, the lesbian writer. For the next three weeks the new writing partnership shifted to the Hamptons in upstate New York, where they finished the songs for the album that would be called *Desire*.

Back in the studio on July 30, with the likes of Emmylou Harris, violinist Scarlett Rivera, bass player Ron Stoner and drummer Howie Wyeth, Dylan completed seven songs for the new album, and on the following day he finished both 'Isis' and 'Sara', two songs about his wife, who was with him at the session.

Desire, Dylan's third successive chart-topping album in America and a number three hit in the UK, also featured the song Dylan and Levy had written about the boxer Rubin 'Hurricane' Carter, who had been arrested for murder in 1966. Dylan held concerts in support of Carter as part of the Rolling Thunder Revue while 'Hurricane' an 11-minute song and a top 50 hit in both the US and the UK, helped the fighter get his conviction overturned in 1985.

Recorded live at Hughes Stadium in Fort Collins, Colorado, on May 23, during the second section of the Rolling Thunder Revue, the release of album *Hard Rain* coincided with the broadcast in September 1976 of an NBC TV special of the same name, sponsored by Craig Powerplay Car Stereo and Audio Components.

After an earlier recording from a Florida show had been rejected, Dylan paid for the Colorado show to be taped on the eve of his 35th birthday. With wife Sara in the audience, the show was a rip-roaring performance which impressed bass player Stone: "It's like a punk record. It's got such energy and anger."

Although it was entitled *Hard Rain*, Dylan's 'A Hard Rain's

Gonna Fall' was missing from the album but was the opening track of the TV show, while he threw in a new arrangement of 'Maggie's Farm' and performed 'Lay Lady Lay' with some raunchy new lyrics. *Hard Rain* peaked at number 17 in America but followed *Desire* to the number three spot in the UK.

After releasing the *Desire* and *Hard Rain* albums Dylan became preoccupied with domestic matters, as Sara successfully filed for divorce in the summer of 1977. He distracted himself with preparations for a world tour and with a new album, which he began after the Japanese and Australian dates were over.

With a group consisting in the main of musicians from his touring band – including Steve Stoner, David Mansfield, Jesse Ed Davis, Ian Wallace, Billy Cross, Bobbye Hall, Steve Douglas and Jerry Scheff – Dylan, using his own Rundown Studio in Los Angeles, cut all nine tracks on the *Street Legal* album in just five days during April 1978. "We couldn't find the right producer so we just brought in the remote truck … and went for a live sound," he said later.

Street Legal got to number 11 in the US but went to number 2 – and was certified platinum – in the UK, where sales were boosted by his arrival in the UK in June 1978 (for the first since 1966) to play six shows at Earls Court plus the Blackbushe Aerodrome festival in July, for which he was reportedly paid a grand total of £650,000.

Hard Rain

Released 1976. Tracks: Maggie's Farm, One Too Many Mornings, Stuck Inside Of Mobile, Oh Sister, Lay Lady Lay, Shelter From The Storm, You're A Big Girl Now, I Threw It All Away, Idiot Wind.

Desire

Released 1976. Tracks: Hurricane, Isis, Mozambique, One More Cup Of Coffee, Oh Sister, Joey, Romance In Durango, Black Diamond Bay, Sara.

ABOVE Dylan on stage during his 1978 *Street Legal* world tour.

RIGHT An original 8-track cassette for 1978's *Street Legal*.

Working with Dylan in the UK was CBS press officer Elly Smith, who recalled delivering some music to his London hotel room. "I wondered if he was aware of the punk thing that was going on so I got some of my records together and put them in his room. I remember writing a note and began worrying whether I should say, 'Dear Mr Dylan', 'Dear Bob' or just 'Bob'."

After Dylan had commented on Smith's leather jacket and asked if she would take him shopping, she received a phone call in her hotel room. "This voice said 'Is that Elly? This is Bob'. He said he'd been listening to the records and wanted me to go to his room and talk about them. He was really interested in the music. I don't think he'd been exposed to very much punk before."

With Dylan making it clear to his record company that he wasn't going to do any interviews or promote *Street Legal* in any way other than by playing his concerts – "Everything on the tour was very disciplined, he was always on time and there were never any tantrums," recalls Smith – it left time for what he liked doing most.

"He wanted to go to gigs so I took him to Dingwalls to see Elvis Costello," says Smith. "I had a pass for me and a guest, but the guy on the door said that there was no room for any guests. Then he looked at my guest, saw it was Bob Dylan and said, 'OK he can come in'." However, a plan to go to Dalston in East London to hear some reggae in a club recommended by The Clash's Joe Strummer was abandoned when the management decided it was too dangerous.

Smith's one lasting disappointment is that while she got Dylan to autograph a bunch of his albums for a competition, she never got a copy signed for herself. "I would really have loved him to have done one for me but I couldn't ask him because I didn't want look like a fan. I was very aware of being professional," says Smith, an American who went on to work at Virgin and Sire.

Street Legal

Released June 1978. Tracks: Changing Of the Guards, New Pony, No Time To Think, Baby Stop Crying, Is Your Love In Vain?, Senor (Tales Of Yankee Power), True Love Tends To Forget, We Better Talk This Over, Where Are You Tonight?.

BELOW LEFT The man behind the shades posing for a 1978 portrait.

BELOW RIGHT Relaxing on the tour bus as they travel through London, 1978.

The Gospel Years

At the end of Dylan's 1978 world tour, the man returned to America to play a further 64 shows spread over 92 days, beginning in Augusta, Georgia, on September 15. Originally dubbed "the alimony tour", it was later called "the Vegas tour" as Dylan was criticized for allegedly running through his greatest hits in a cabaret-style set.

In response to suggestions that he'd gone cabaret or even disco, Dylan said: "I don't know how they come up with these theories. We never heard them when we played Australia, Japan or Europe." Much of the bad press had been prompted by his baffling film *Renaldo and Clara* and the less-than-perfect *Street Legal* album.

One man who crossed Dylan's path during the US tour was Keith Emerson, keyboard player with ELP, who played the same venue one day after Dylan. "The promoter invited me to go to a hotel suite where there was to be a party," recalls Emerson. "I sat around for about 45 minutes after Bob's performance and there was no sign of the great man until he came in, walked right past everyone and went into his bedroom."

Persuaded by the promoter not to leave, Emerson finally got to meet Dylan and recalls how the conversation went. "Bob said, 'Where you from?' and I said, 'England; where you from?' He sort of nodded in a northerly direction. We both realized it wasn't going to be a very scintillating conversation. Bob shrugged his shoulders and I went to my room wondering what all that had been about."

In the middle of his American dates, Dylan played a gig in San Diego in November while feeling unwell. "I think the crowd could see that. And they threw a silver cross on the stage," said Dylan, who rarely collected things thrown by the audience. "I picked up the cross and I put it my pocket and I brought it to the next town, which was in Arizona ... I was feeling even worse. I said 'I need something tonight that I didn't have before' and I looked in my pocket and I had this cross."

Dylan would later explain that in his hotel room in Tucson, Arizona, he had a vision of Christ. "Jesus did appear to me as King of Kings and Lord of Lords," he said "There was a presence in the room that couldn't have been anybody but Jesus." Slowly, with the same silver cross around his neck, Dylan began to change the lyrics of his songs to include Bible references, and as the tour drew to its close he began writing songs that would reflect his new-found conversion to Christianity.

Dylan had also begun to attend courses at the Vineyard Fellowship, a Christian organization based in California, before he went into the famous Muscle Shoals studio in Miami to start recording at the end of April 1979. He recruited Dire Straits guitarist Mark Knopfler and legendary producer Jerry Wexler to work on the album alongside

ABOVE and TOP By 1979 Dylan's shows had begun to reflect his move to Christianity.

RIGHT Performing with his 'heavenly choir' during the tours for *Slow Train Coming* and *Saved*.

Slow Train Coming

Released 1979. Tracks: Gotta Serve Somebody, Precious Angel, I Believe In You, Slow Train, Gonna Change My Way Of Thinking, Do Right To Me Babe (Do Unto Others), When You Gonna Wake Up?, Man Gave Names To All The Animals, When He Returns.

drummer Pick Withers, keyboardist (and co-producer) Barry Beckett, bassist Tim Drummond, singers Carolyn Dennis and Helena Springs plus the famous Muscle Shoals Horns.

Between April 30 and May 11 they worked their way through nine songs, finishing up with 'When He Returns', which closed the album, called Slow Train Coming, and featured Dylan's hastily rehearsed lead vocal over Beckett's piano track.

'Gotta Save Somebody' displayed Dylan's new enthusiasm for rock gospel singing and the top 30 US single earned him the 1980 Grammy Award for Best Rock Vocal Performance.

The track 'Slow Train' was a song which Dylan debuted at a sound check for a show near the end of his 1978 US tour and came close to alienating many of his fans, who suspected their man of something akin to American jingoism.

Slow Train Coming took Dylan back into the US top three, and in the UK it followed *Street Legal* to the number two spot.

Dylan was back at Muscle Shoals just nine months after making *Slow Train Coming*, in February 1980, and once again Wexler and Beckett were in charge of production for the sessions, which featured Beckett, Dennis and Drummond alongside drummer Jim Keltner and Spooner Oldham on keyboards.

The nine songs on *Saved* continued Dylan's Christian theme following his religious conversion, with one review saying the album was an "open declaration of Dylan's deepening faith." While Dylan composed seven of the tracks, he co-wrote the title track with Drummond and opened the album with a 1950s country classic. 'A Satisfied Mind' was written by Red Hayes and Jack Rhodes, and covered by both Ella Fitzgerald and The Byrds, but the high spot was Porter Wagoner's 1955 version, which topped the US country chart.

Dylan's 20th studio album, Saved was not a commercial success in America, where it peaked at number 24 (his first album since *Another Side Of Bob Dylan* in 1964 not to reach the top 20) but it went to number three in the UK and became his tenth successive top 10 album.

Saved
Released 1980. Tracks: A Satisfied Mind, Saved, Covenant Woman, What Can I Do For You?, Solid Rock, Pressing On, In the Garden, Saving Grace, Are You Ready?

The wilderness years

In 1981 Dylan completed his trilogy of religious albums with the release of *Shot of Love*, which also showed the first signs of his return to secular songs. It continued his run of UK top 10 albums, peaking at number 6, but missed the top 30 in America despite Dylan's assertion that it was the "most explosive" album he'd made.

While many critics didn't agree, Dylan still set off on his *Shot of Love* tour of America, proving that he could still fill auditoriums across the country. By the time he came to record *Infidels* in 1983 Dylan's religious fervour was on the wane, although he chose to release an album with just eight tracks while discarding a further eight including 'Blind Willie McTell', his tribute to the blues musician.

Co-produced with Mark Knopfler and featuring former Rolling Stones guitarist Mick Taylor, *Infidels* boasted the single 'Jokerman' which, despite Dylan being persuaded to make his first video for MTV, failed to chart in either the UK or the US. The album, however, was a bestseller, reaching number 20 in America and becoming another UK top 10 hit – his 23rd.

Dylan was back on the road in 1984 and three shows – recorded in Dublin, London and Newcastle – formed his *Real Live* album release. Critics called the choice of songs "hopeless," described the performances as "inadequate" and panned the productions as "inexcusable," even though he was backed by Taylor, Faces' keyboardist Ian McLagan and guitarist Carlos Santana. The ten-track collection missed the UK top 50 and also failed to enter the US Top 100.

Fresh from taking part in the USA For Africa recording of 'We Are The World' in January 1985, Dylan returned to the studios to embark on *Empire Burlesque* with the help of famed dance producer Arthur Baker, who had worked with Bruce Springsteen and Cyndi Lauper and suggested Dylan hired him in order to make him sound "a little more contemporary."

The album ranged from rock to ballads, including an acoustic track, with some studio trickery thrown in, and ignited renewed public interest in Dylan's recordings, hitting the US top 40 and missing the UK Top 10 by just one place.

After closing the US Live Aid event in Philadelphia in July 1985 – backed by Stones' guitarists Keith Richards and Ronnie Wood – and issuing his five-album box set *Biograph* (with its 18 unreleased tracks), Dylan spent parts of both 1985 and 1986 in the studio working on the album *Knocked Out Loaded*.

Eventually recorded in London and produced by The Eurythmics' Dave Stewart, it featured just eight songs, including covers of 'You

ABOVE Bob Dylan considers the sounds of the 1980s.

ABOVE Four Wilburys (l to r): Dylan, Tom Petty, Jeff Lynne and George Harrison.

BELOW Sharing the vocals with Tom Petty.

Wanna Ramble', 'They Killed Him' and 'Precious Memories', along with tracks left off his previous album. 'Brownsville Girl', co-written with playwright Sam Shepard, was an 11-minute track in the best tradition of his earlier epic songs. Even so, the album only just crept into the UK top 40 and failed to chart in America.

Dylan, who had married singer Carolyn Dennis in 1986, was still a major artist for Columbia where Walter Yetnikoff was president of the CBS label division. He recalled hosting a post-concert dinner party for Dylan in New York in the mid-Eighties but at 2am there was no sign of the star. "(Then) just like that he and his entourage walked through the door. I was expecting Bohemian groupies and scruffy musicians. Instead he arrived with his family – his Jewish uncles, Jewish cousins and Jewish mother."

All this came as no surprise to Yetnikoff, who had dealt with artists throughout his long music business career. "As much as you could deal with Dylan, I dealt with him. I understood how hard he worked to protect his mystique. He was entitled," he said. "I saw him as a master poet, master folk rocker, voice of a generation, American icon and a guy who still sold a shitload of records."

Dylan spent much of 1987 touring, firstly in America with The Grateful Dead and then in Europe with members of Tom Petty's band The Heartbreakers. He also went into the studio, cutting the album *Down In The Groove* which, for many, proved he was struggling to be a contemporary 1980s artist. He filled the albums with covers of early songs by Hank Snow, the Stanley Brothers and Wilbert Harrison, plus 'Sally Sue Brown' (released in 1960 by Arthur Alexander), which he recorded with former Clash man Paul Simonon and ex-Sex Pistol Steve Jones.

Down In The Groove was a top 40 hit in the UK but was surpassed in 1989 by the album *Dylan And The Dead*, when Dylan and the band he'd toured with in 1987 got together to record versions of seven Dylan songs including 'Slow Train', 'All Along The Watchtower' and 'Knockin' On Heaven's Door'. The collection returned Dylan to the US top 40 and continued his run of UK top 40 hits.

Dylan's induction into the Rock and Roll Hall of Fame in January 1989 – when Bruce Springsteen told the audience in New York: "Bob freed your mind in the way Elvis freed your body" – followed his decision in 1988 to join George Harrison, Jeff Lynne, Roy Orbison and Tom Petty as a member of The Travelin' Wilburys. Their debut album *Volume One* was a US top three hit while the single 'Handle With Care' reached number 21 in the UK.

RIGHT With Ronnie Wood (l) and Keith Richards of the Rolling Stones during US Live Aid.

BELOW Dylan goes down to the river after a difficult decade.

Oh Mercy

Despite all the travails and turbulence of the Eighties, Dylan managed to end the most difficult decade of his career with his most successful and most acclaimed album for years.

Oh Mercy was recorded in the spring of 1989 and signaled his first association with U2's producer Daniel Lanois, who recalled his first experience of working with Dylan. "I sat next to him for two months while he wrote the album and it was extraordinary. He keeps chipping away at his verses."

Lanois had been recommended by U2's Bono, and Dylan remembered his meeting with the French-Canadian producer. "Daniel came to see me when we were playing New Orleans and … we hit it off. He had an understanding of what my music was all about." Getting together with Lanois also enabled Dylan to experience the producer's portable studio, set up in an old colonial house in New Orleans where he was recording The Neville Brothers' album *Yellow Moon*, which featured Dylan's 'Ballad of Hollis Brown' and 'With God On Our Side'.

Taken with the idea of recording in New Orleans, Dylan returned to the city in the spring of 1989 armed with half a dozen songs which dated back to late 1987 and early 1988. Apparently he had shown some of them to George Harrison during The Travelin' Wilburys' sessions and the ex-Beatle urged Dylan to write more and then record them.

The studio in New Orleans was located in a building with, according to Lanois, "a bordello overtone" which was enhanced with moss, stuffed animals and alligator heads. Reluctant to use his touring band, Dylan relied on his new producer to recruit local musicians such as guitarists Mason Ruffner and Brian Stoltz, bassist Tony Hall and drummer Willie Green, while Lanois added dobro, guitar and pedal steel and engineer Malcolm Burn joined in on tambourine, keyboards and bass.

The ten songs that finally made it on to *Oh Mercy* were initially recorded during March and April 1989, before Dylan headed off on another trip to Europe: but before he left the first signs of tension between artist and producer had begun to appear.

Different versions of songs were recorded and discarded, while a local zydeco band were hired but eventually rejected and at one point Dylan despaired over Lanois' treatment of a song called 'Dignity', which missed the album's final track listing. "Whatever promise Dan had seen in the song was beaten into a bloody mess," he said.

FAR RIGHT Dylan hits Rotterdam in Holland during a European tour.

BELOW RIGHT Dylan and The Grateful Dead join up during a US tour.

LEFT Dylan adopts a Mexican look for a new decade of touring and recording.

RIGHT Another year older and another new image.

During the recording sessions Dylan was also busy writing more songs, and by the end of his time in New Orleans he had around 14 or 15 songs recorded and ready for consideration, despite the continuing friction with Lanois. Explaining that he was pretty much set in his ways, Dylan said "There wasn't much chance in changing now. I didn't need to climb the next mountain." Reflecting on the finished album, he said: "There'd been a clashing of spirits at times but nothing that had turned into a bitter or complicated struggle. I can't say if it's the record either of us wanted."

'Man In A Long Black Coat' has its roots deep in America's folk music history, and Dylan has been quick to acknowledge Lanois' role in the recording. "Like Sam Phillips (the founder of Sun Records who discovered and produced Elvis Presley) he likes to push artists to the psychological edge and he'd done that with me but he didn't have to do any of that with this song."

'Everything Is Broken' was first recorded early on in the New Orleans sessions as 'Broken Days' but by April, a month after the first version, Dylan had rewritten it and given it a new title.

"Lanois thought it was a throwaway," recalled Dylan in his autobiography, "but I didn't think it was, but there was only one way to find out, only one way to cut it – one style and with plenty of tremolo. I thought the song did just what it had to do."

The first recording of 'Where Teardrops Fall', according to Dylan, "took about five minutes and it wasn't rehearsed" and featured local musician Rockin' Dopsie and his zydeco band, whose other work on the album had been rejected. Despite later efforts, Dylan returned to the original version for the album and exclaimed: "It was just a three-minute ballad but it made you stand straight up and stay right where you were. The song was beautiful and magical, upbeat and it was complete."

The final version of *Oh Mercy* was released in September 1989 and restored Dylan to the US top 30 for the first time since 1980, while in the UK, after six low chart entries, Dylan found himself back in the Top 10, at number six.

Oh Mercy
Released 1989. Tracks: Political World, Where Teardrops Fall, Everything Is Broken, Ring Them Bells, Man In The Long Black Coat, Most Of The Time, What Good Am I?, Disease Of Conceit, What Was It You Wanted, Shooting Star.

Into the 1990s

In the wake of *Oh Mercy* Dylan opened the new decade with a festival in Brazil plus guest spots at a Roy Orbison tribute for the homeless, with Bruce Springsteen and Tom Petty and finally alongside Bono, Van Morrison and Nina Simone on various European dates.

He also went back into the studio in spring 1990 to start new album *Under The Red Sky*. Lanois was replaced as producer by Don and David Was, plus Dylan himself (under the name Jack Frost), and they were joined by the largest array of superstars Dylan had ever assembled – George Harrison, Elton John, Slash from Guns N'Roses, Stevie Ray Vaughan, David Crosby and Bruce Hornsby.

For some reason Dylan took to wearing a hooded sweatshirt throughout recording, which left a lasting impression on Slash. "I finally met this guy who looked like an Eskimo … he's wearing a heavy wool sweater with a hood and baseball cap underneath," he said before adding: "He was really impolite. I didn't really have a good time."

In 2006, Dylan explained the album was a hurried affair interrupted by his Traveling Wilburys work, and there were too many people in the studio. It was dedicated to "Gabby Goo Goo," which it transpired was Dylan's nickname for his four-year-old daughter.

Two songs, 'Born In Time' and 'God Knows', were left over from the Oh Mercy sessions while 'TV Talkin' Song' was inspired by a visit to Speakers' Corner in London's Hyde Park. Harrison appeared on the title track, while Slash provided guitar on 'Wiggle Wiggle' and John piano on 'Two By Two'.

The album peaked at a disappointing number 38 in the US but a healthier number 13 in the UK.

Having been recognized in France in 1990 by being made a Commandeur de l'Ordre des Arts et des Lettres, and with a Lifetime Achievement award at the 1991 Grammy Awards, Dylan celebrated his own 30th year in the record business with a concert at New York's Madison Square Garden in October 1992, featuring the likes of Harrison, Petty, Eric Clapton, Johnny Cash, Stevie Wonder, Richie Havens and Willie Nelson.

Reflecting on his career the year before, Dylan had said: "Maybe a person gets to the point where they've written enough songs," but it didn't stop him returning to the studio in summer 1992 to embark on a new album, but this time without any original Dylan songs. *Good As I Been To You* emerged from a set of acoustic folk recordings made with David Bromberg as producer, which Dylan scrapped but later re-worked with producer Debbie Gold in his Malibu garage studio.

Dylan was the only musician credited – on vocals, guitar and

ABOVE In Spain in 1991 and Dylan plays duelling guitars with Keith Richards of the Rolling Stones.

Under The Red Sky
Released 1990. Tracks: Wiggle Wiggle, Under The Red Sky, Unbelievable, Born In Time, TV Talkin' Song, 10,000 Men, Two By Two, God Knows, Handy Dandy, Cat's In The Well

harmonica – and he focused on recording a number of traditional songs, including the opening track 'Frankie and Albert', his own version of a Mississippi John Hurt song previously covered by Jerry Lee Lewis and Gene Vincent, and 'Tomorrow Night', which had been recorded by Elvis Presley and Lonnie Johnson.

Credited as arranger on all 13 tracks, Dylan also offered up 'Diamond Joe', a Western ballad covered by his old Sixties folk friends Ramblin' Jack Elliott and Tom Rush, and 'Black Jack Davey', which he was taped singing in 1961. He finished up with a glorious six-minute version of the children's favourite 'Froggie Went A-Courtin'.'

Dylan described the songs on the album, which reached number 51 in America and crept into the UK top 20 – as "the music that's true to me."

Before he began work on his next album Dylan continued with his extraordinary round of live work, which took in numerous guest appearances including joining Willie Nelson on stage and on his *Across The Borderline* album, in addition to visiting the UK (again) for a week of shows and debuting at the New Orleans Jazz and Heritage Festival.

He returned to the studio in his Malibu home in May 1993 to record a second collection of traditional folk songs, which he performed acoustically on guitar and harmonica and also produced. In fact, he recorded a total of 14 songs in a matter of a few days and focused on simple and often basic recording techniques in an effort to retain an authentic feel on *World Gone Wrong*.

It featured songs like 'Ragged and Dirty', recorded by Sleepy John Estes in the 1920s and later by Willie Brown, and 'Broke Down Engine', which came from Blind Willie McTell. Title track 'World Gone Wrong' was inspired by a 1930s version by the Mississippi Sheiks, 'Delia' was a song about a murder, which Dylan performed in Minneapolis when he was working the Dinkytown folk clubs, while 'Stack A Lee' dated back to 1928 and Cliff Edwards.

The album, which featured a cover photograph taken in a restaurant in London's Camden Town, gained a modest number 70 placing in the US and a disappointing number 35 in the UK, although it did earn him a Grammy for Best Traditional Folk Album.

CLOCKWISE FROM TOP LEFT Dressing in contemporary youth style; Dylan collected his French cultural medal in Paris in 1990; Dylan shares a table with Dave Stewart at the Fluke's Cradle restaurant in Camden Town, London.

Enclosures:

item 14 Punched ticket for Bob Dylan at The Supper Club, NYC, November 17, 1993.

item 15 A flyer advertising the Bob Dylan and Paul Simon Hollywood Bowl concert of June 22, 1999.

item 16 Invite to 'An Evening With Bob Dylan', 2000.

item 17 Bob Dylan original setlist.

item 18 Bob Dylan sticker.

item 19 Promo flyer for Dylan's concert in St Etienne, France, 2004.

Good As I Been To You

Released 1992. Tracks: Frankie and Albert, Jim Jones, Black Jack Davey, Canadee-I-O, Sittin' On Top Of The World, Little Maggie, Hard Times, Step It Up And Go, Tomorrow Night, Arthur McBride, You're Gonna Quit Me, Diamond Joe, Froggie Went A-Courtin'

World Gone Wrong

Released 1993. Tracks: World Gone Wrong, Love Henry, Ragged and Dirty, Blood In My Eyes, Broke Down Engine, Delia, Stack A Lee, Two Soldiers, Jack-A-Roe, Lone Pilgrim

A Return to Form

Dylan's obsession with performing live may have taken the edge off his interest in recording an album of new material. In 1991, after he released *Under The Red Sky*, his last album of new material, Dylan admitted in an interview: "There was a time when songs would come three or four at the same time but those days are long gone."

After his two albums of traditional American folk music, Dylan went back on the road for his own dates and also continued with his habit of duetting along the way; he sang with The Rolling Stones and Bruce Springsteen, and even performed 'Restless Farewell' at a celebration for Frank Sinatra's 80th birthday.

One other date that stood out in his itinerary was the so-called Woodstock II festival, held in August 1994 to mark the 25th anniversary of the original event which Dylan had ignored. This time he travelled to a new site on Winston Farm in Saugerties, New York, to play a 12-song, 78- minute set in front of 250,000 people for a reported fee of $600,000.

In 1996 news filtered through that Dylan was busy on his farm in Minnesota writing a fresh set of songs and in January 1997, when he entered the Criteria Studios in Miami, Florida, to begin recording officially, the producer chosen to work on his 30th studio album was Daniel Lanois, the man behind the hit title *Oh Mercy*.

The musicians assembled for the album included slide guitarist Cindy Cashdollar, drummers Brian Blade and Jim Keltner, guitarists Bob Britt and Duke Robillard plus pianist Jim Dickinson and former Sir Douglas Quintet organist Augie Meyers, while Dylan (again using the name Jack Frost) acted as co-producer on the 11 new songs he chose for the double album.

However, it seems relations between artist and producer were once again pushed to the limit as the band recorded the album live in the studio, with Dylan apparently re-working and editing songs as he went along. Lanois later commented: "Well, you never know what you're going to get. He's an eccentric man," while pianist Dickinson recalled: "Twelve musicians playing live – three sets of drums … it was unbelievable – two pedal steels." He later added that at the end of the album even the musicians weren't sure "who's playing what".

Auger's ghostly organ sound was predominant on the album's opening track 'Love Sick', together with Dylan's slightly unworldly

RIGHT Bob Dylan takes to the stage sporting some fancy embroidery and a cowboy hat.

vocal. He later explained: "It's a spooky record because I feel spooky," and then agreed to it being used in a TV advert for the lingerie store Victoria's Secret (featuring his image and some scantily clad models), while 'Tryin' To Get To Heaven' was a step on from his classic 'Knockin' On' Heaven's Door', and bizarrely hinted at events that would occur later in the year.

According to the revered singer Emmylou Harris, the song 'Not Dark Yet' is the finest work ever written about growing old. "For those of us entering that door, it brings up things we didn't know we were capable of feeling", she said after the album was released.

Not for the first time, Dylan finished the album with the longest track available, and the 16-minute epic 'Highlands' again has a sense of fatality about it with Dylan's eerie commentary namechecking the likes of Erica Jong and Neil Young.

After the completion of the album *Time Out Of Mind* in January 1997 and before its eventual release in September, Dylan fell seriously ill with a heart disorder caused by a fungal infection. He was taken into hospital in the last week of May 1997 and, after a week long stay, was sent home to rest for six months. "I really thought I'd be seeing Elvis soon," was his observation.

By the time the album came out, however, he was back on the road – during the following year he would play 133 live shows – and reflected on *Time Out Of Mind* to *Guitar World* in 1999: "It doesn't take itself seriously, but then again the sound is very significant to that record. There wasn't any wasted effort on *Time Out Of Mind*." The critics were also impressed with the album's sound, *NME* declaring: "The original is back," while *The Guardian* decided he was "at his creative peak" and *Newsweek* magazine ran the headline "Dylan lives", and featured him on the front cover for the first time in 23 years.

While single releases 'Not Dark Yet' and 'Love Sick' failed to make any real impression, *Time Out Of Mind* reached number 10 in both the US (where it was certified platinum) and the UK. It also brought him his best haul of Grammy Awards, being voted Album of the Year and Best Contemporary Folk Album while the song 'Cold Irons Bound' was rated Best Male Rock Vocal Performance. The ceremony in January 1998 became a family affair when Dylan's son Jakob and his band Wallflowers won two Grammys for Best Rock Song and Best Rock Performance by a Group.

> ### *Time Out Of Mind*
> Released 1997. Tracks: Love Sick, Dirt Road Blues, Standing In The Doorway, Million Miles, Tryin' To Get To Heaven, 'Til I Fell In Love With You, Not Dark Yet, Cold Irons Bound, Make You Feel My Love, Can't Wait, Highlands.

ABOVE RIGHT Together with Bruce 'The Boss' Springsteen at the Rock And Roll Hall of Fame in 1995.

RIGHT Dylan was joined on stage at the 1998 Grammy Awards by protesting dancer Michael Portnay.

Love And Theft and Modern Times

Between albums Dylan was once again on the road, this time sharing the bill with Van Morrison, stepping out as support for The Rolling Stones, touring the US with both Morrison and Joni Mitchell, making his debut at Glastonbury, performing in Australia with Patti Smith and playing nearly 50 shows across America with Paul Simon.

Somewhere along the way he also penned a new song, 'Things Have Changed', for the soundtrack to the film *Wonder Boys*, starring Michael Douglas. In 2001 it won the Oscar for Best Song and he told The Times: "A lot of performers have won Grammys but very few have won Academy Awards, so that puts me on a different plateau."

On May 24, 2001, his 60th birthday, Dylan was in the studio in New York working on a new album with his regular backing band of Larry Campbell (guitar/violin/banjo), Charlie Sexton (guitar), Tony Garnier (bass) and David Kemper (drums), plus organist and accordionist Augie Meyers. Again under the name Jack Frost, Dylan produced the *Love And Theft* album, completed between May 9 and 26 and described by Dylan as "autobiographical on every front."

Opening track 'Tweedle Dee and Tweedle Dum' has its heart in the Mardi Gras carnivals of New Orleans and features Clay Meyers on bongos. It's followed by 'Mississippi', a song Dylan offered to Sheryl Crow, who recorded it in 1998 before Dylan, having left it off *Time Out Of Mind*, decided to revisit the song.

'High Water (For Charley Patton)' was a tribute to the legendary Delta blues singer who grew up alongside Leadbelly and Robert Johnson and inspired Dylan. He had used Patton's songs on earlier albums and this song refers directly to Patton's 1929 recording 'High Water Everywhere' about the Mississippi floods of 1927.

Love And Theft was unforgettably released on September 11, 2001 – the day of the terrorist attacks on the World Trade Center in New York and the Pentagon in Washington D.C. – and received an array of five-star reviews, reaching number five in the US and number three in the UK.

After *Love And Theft* the world had to wait a further five years for the next instalment in Dylan's recording career. But while he continued on his merry way around America, Europe and Asia,

ABOVE The musician entertaining, circa 2006.

RIGHT On stage in Denmark as the Dylan traveling show hit Europe in 2001.

Love And Theft
Released September 2001. Tracks: Tweedle Dee and Tweedle Dum, Mississippi, Summer Days, Bye And Bye, Lonesome Day Blues, Floater (Too Much To Ask), High Water (For Charley Patton), Moonlight, Honest With Me, Po' Boy, Cry A While, Sugar Baby

he was also putting the finishing touches to the first volume of his autobiography, watching 15 of his albums being remastered and reissued and also hosting his own *Theme Time* radio show.

Early in 2006 he assembled his touring band – regular bass player Garnier was now joined by drummer George G. Receli, guitarists Stu Kimball and Denny Freeman, plus Donnie Herron on steel guitar, violin and mandolin – for a series of rehearsals in the Bardavon 1869 Opera House in Poughkeepsie, New York. Before the end of February, they transferred to Clinton Studios in Manhattan to start and finish the album *Modern Times* in less than three weeks with Dylan again producing as Jack Frost.

While the ten songs were all credited as Dylan originals, there was controversy over the origins of some. The opening track 'Thunder On the Mountain' was alleged to contain a second verse based on Ma Rainey's song 'Memphis Minnie', although Dylan bizarrely replaced the reference to Ma Rainey with a namecheck for Alicia Keys.

It was followed by the blues standard 'Rollin' And Tumblin'' – recorded by Hambone Willie Newbern and Muddy Waters, who has also been credited with composing the song – with new Dylan lyrics after the original first verse.

'Workingman's Blues #2' can be traced to songs by jazz singer June Christy ('June's Blues'), Willie Dixon ('Down In the Bottom') and Big Joe Williams ('Meet Me Around The Corner').

Talking to *Los Angeles Times* writer Robert Hilburn, he appeared unconcerned by the furore over his use of old songs. "I'll take a song I know and simply start playing it in my head. That's the way I meditate," he said. "I'm listening to a song in my head. At a certain point, some words will change and I'll start writing a new song." In 1999, he told *Guitar World*: "I've got 500, 600, 700 songs. I don't have a problem with the backlog of songs. Some fade away and diminish in time and others take their place."

Whether the songs on *Modern Times* were old or new, Dylan originals or adaptations seems to have made no difference to his fans or the critics, who gave it five-star reviews. *Modern Times* became Dylan's first US number one since *Desire* in 1976 and earned him the distinction, at 65, of being the oldest living artist to enter the chart in the top spot. Despite hitting number one in Canada, Australia, Denmark and Norway, it peaked at number three in the UK but passed the six million sales mark worldwide.

Placed at number one in *Rolling Stone* magazine's list of the 50 Greatest Albums of 2006, *Modern Times* also brought Dylan two more Grammys: for Best Contemporary Folk/Americana Album and Best Rock Vocal Performance for 'Someday Baby'.

BELOW Dylan toured the US and Europe with Irish singer Van Morrison.

BOTTOM He appeared at the 2010 Academy Awards via satellite link from Sydney.

Together Through Life and Christmas In The Heart

In the three years between the award-winning *Modern Times* and his next studio venture, Dylan spent time on his farm in Minnesota, at his Malibu house in California, and in a host of hotel rooms as he continued in his role as the wandering minstrel.

By the time he returned to recording, he had found a new songwriting partner in The Grateful Dead's lyricist Robert Hunter. They had collaborated on two tracks on Dylan's largely ignored 1988 album *Down In The Groove* and this new partnership represented Dylan's first major co-writing exercise since Jacques Levy and *Desire*.

As the album *Together Through Life* began to evolve in December 2008, Dylan recruited The Heartbreakers' guitarist/mandolin player Mike Campbell and guitarist/accordionist David Hildago (from Los Lobos) to join regular band members Garnier (bass), Recile (drums) and Herron (steel guitar/banjo/trumpet). As Jack Frost, he was still in charge of production as the ten tracks took shape.

It seems Dylan's inspiration to make a new album was French film director Olivier Dahan, who asked him to contribute to his movie *My Own Love Song*. Dylan came up with a song, but recalled: "The record sort of took its own direction" after Dahan asked for a whole soundtrack. Dylan also spoke about Hunter, saying: "We could probably write a hundred songs together if we thought it was important or the right reasons were there … He's got a way with words and I do too."

As it was, the pair wrote eight of the album's ten songs, with Dylan adding to Willie Dixon's 'My Wife's Home Town' while 'This Dream Of You' was his only solo song on the album. It was released in April 2009 with little fanfare or advance publicity. Anticipating the reaction, coming as it did after his number one, Grammy-winning *Modern Times*, Dylan reported on his website: "I know my fans will like it. Other than that I have no idea."

He quickly found out the critics were also impressed, one BBC commentator calling it "a masterful reading of 20th-century American folk" while *Mojo* magazine assessed it as "dark yet comforting." Others too gave it a five-star rating, and the fans made *Together Through Life* Dylan's second successive US number one

Together Through Life

Released 2009. Tracks: Beyond Here Lies Nothin', Life Is Hard, My Wife's Home Town, If You Ever Go To Houston, Forgetful Heart, Jolene, This Dream Of You, Shake Shake Mama, I Feel a Change Comin' On, It's All Good

RIGHT Dylan hits all the right notes during one of his 2009 live shows.

album while in the UK it earned him the top spot for the first time since 1970's *New Morning*.

Having recorded protest songs, love songs, folk songs and children's songs, it was still a surprise when Dylan produced a collection of traditional Christmas songs, even if it was to aid charities, with royalties going to Feed America, the United Nations' World Food Programme and Crisis in the UK.

Some time in May 2009 Dylan assembled regulars Garnier, Herron and Recile from his touring band and added Hildago plus guitarist Phil Upchurch, keyboard player Patrick Warren and seven backing singers. With Jack Frost still in charge, they assembled in Jackson Browne's studio in Santa Monica, California, to bring to life a collection of 15 hymns, carols and seasonal standards.

Although Jewish by birth, Dylan explained, Christmas was "so worldwide and everybody can relate to it in their own way." Asked why he performed them straight, without any of his usual quirkiness, he said: "There wasn't any other way to play it. These songs are part of my life, just like folk songs."

With tracks ranging from 'Winter Wonderland' (a 1957 hit for Johnny Mathis), 'Little Drummer Boy' (recorded by David Bowie with Bing Crosby in 1982) and 'Have Yourself A Merry Little Christmas' (made famous by Judy Garland in 1944 and Frank Sinatra in 1957) to 'Hark The Herald Angels Sing' and

'O Come All Ye Faithful' plus 'O' Little Town of Bethlehem' and 'Here Comes Santa Claus', *Christmas In The Heart* was a delightful enigma to most people.

A BBC review suggested fans "indulge Dylan's whims" as the record was "worth a spin come Christmas morn," while Richard Williams in *The Guardian* noted: "The result is polished without being glib and sympathetic listeners may find it addictive," before adding: "It seems safe to say, however, that no one has ever tackled 'O Come All Ye Faithful' quite like this."

To support the album's release in October 2009, Dylan even made a video for the single 'Must Be Santa', in which he portrayed a Father Christmas character – half Dickensian, half punk – at a seasonal house party which erupts into fighting and mayhem. It made it to number 41 in the UK.

Christmas In the Heart topped both Billboard's US Holiday and Folk album charts while peaking at 23 in the overall chart and reaching number ten in the UK. Significantly, Dylan signed off an interview by saying: "Even at this point in time they (the critics) still don't know what to make of me."

Christmas In the Heart
released 2009. Tracks: Here Comes Santa Claus, Do You Hear What I Hear?, Winter Wonderland, Hark The Herald Angels Sing, I'll Be Home For Christmas, Little Drummer Boy, The Christmas Blues, O Come, All Ye Faithful, Have Yourself A Merry Little Christmas, Must Be Santa, Silver Bells, The First Noel, Christmas Island, The Christmas Song, O Little Town Of Bethlehem

RIGHT Nearly 70 years old and still in the spotlight.

BELOW In 2010 Dylan took his Never Ending Tour to Japan, South Korea, Europe and the US.

The Never Ending Tour

Dylan spent the month before his 71st birthday (May 24, 2012) playing dates in Brazil, Argentina and Chile. It was the latest leg of what has been dubbed the "Never Ending Tour," although the man himself questions the title, asking: "Does anybody call Henry Ford a never-ending car builder?"

By all accounts the "NET" started with a concert in the Pavilion in Concord, California, on June 7, 1988, and the 20th and 21st centuries' ultimate troubadour has been circling the globe ever since. The roots of the longest tour in rock history lie in Dylan's association with The Grateful Dead and their philosophy that music is all about playing live rather than recording – something Dylan took on board after he played with The Dead in early 1988.

Averaging more than 100 dates a year, regularly taking in America, Canada, Europe, Japan, Australia, New Zealand and South America – he included Israel, China and South-East Asia in 2011 – Dylan explained: "I knew I've got to go out and play these songs. You just don't have to start it up and end it. It's better just to keep it out there."

Once he got over his less than enthusiastic reception in 1966, Dylan maintained a healthy relationship with the UK, regularly including it in his itinerary between 1978 and 1987, the year before the "NET" began, when CBS UK chairman Paul Russell faced a particular challenge.

"He was playing Wembley and we had a platinum disc that I wanted to give to him," says Russell. "We put together a small gathering of around 20 people – top retailers, top broadcasters who had helped his career – and invited them to come backstage."

However, when Russell was told Dylan wouldn't attend the presentation, he was forced into action. "We'd invited these people so it was difficult to cancel. I went to Wembley early on the day of the show and spoke to Dylan's manager, who said: 'He doesn't do presentations'. I said I wanted to see Bob to talk about it and the manager said: 'He's in that room down there with a couple of his mates so why don't you go and talk to him? Good luck'."

Russell knocked and went in. "There was Bob with Ringo Starr and George Harrison. I explained why I was there and said it'd take him 30 seconds to take the disc and have a photo taken. He said: 'I don't want to do it. I don't do record presentations'. Then Ringo said: 'Bob, don't be a c**t – everybody has to do these things', and Bob looked over at George, who just said that it went with the territory.

"So Bob did it. He walked in, put his arm round my shoulder, didn't even touch the disc, had his picture taken and then walked out the door. And I've still got the picture," says Russell, proudly.

While Simply Red's Mick Hucknall appreciates Dylan's influence on a generation of rock musicians, he has deliberately avoided seeing him live. "I've never seen him in concert. I hear nothing but bad reviews so I've never actually bothered because I didn't want to be disappointed."

On the other hand, Cockney Rebel leader Steve Harley, who covered Dylan's 'Love Minus Zero/No Limit' on his 1996 album *Poetic Justice*, waited until the mid-Nineties before going to see the man who "changed my whole outlook on life in early 1963. I was inspired by the imagery of his songs – it grabbed me."

At the Phoenix Festival in Stratford-on-Avon in 1995, Harley had his own close-up moment. A backstage guest, he was in the hospitality marquee after watching Dylan's performance from the wings – "It's never the best place to see a show but it was a privilege" – when Dylan and his band wandered in.

"He was in his espadrilles and his hoodie, and when they got up to leave Bob was at the back of the line, just at my shoulder. I thought: 'I can't let this moment go', and, as Dylan had changed my life since the age of 12, why would I let this moment go without saying something?

"I stood up and put my hand out. He looked at me and I said: 'Hi; I'm Steve Harley', and he said 'Hey, man' – it was recognition. He sat with me and my two pals, kept his head down, just nodding every now and again but saying nothing. It wasn't a conversation and after ten minutes I was running out of things to say.

"He'd had enough and was getting up to leave when I said something about the heavy rain that was falling and that it was a good job he didn't have to play his set in the rain. He looked at me – for the second time – and just said 'The weather, the weather', and walked off."

By the end of 2011 Dylan and his band had completed close to 2,500 shows on the "Never Ending Tour" with, according to a fan's log, 'Mr Tambourine Man' the most performed song, followed by 'Highway 61 Revisited' and 'Tangled Up In Blue'.

While some performances have been described as "unpredictable" and his lyrics as "effectively unrecognizable", Dylan has shown no sign of ending his gigantic jaunt around the world but he once told the *LA Times*: "I could stop any time … I can see an end to everything, really."

BELOW LEFT Some fancy head gear for Dylan and his band members during their 2010 tour.

BOTTOM A rare photo of Dylan at a disc presentation by Paul Russell of CBS/Sony in 1987.

BELOW and RIGHT "Better just to keep it out there" is Dylan's motto as the show rolls on.